高职高专汽车类规划教材
国家技能型人才培养培训系列教材

汽车实用英语

QICHE SHIYONG YINGYU

吴喜骊　蒋芳　编著

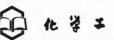
化学工业出版社
·北　京·

内 容 简 介

本书以汽车专业知识和公共英语知识为基础，以训练汽车英文文献的阅读、翻译能力为目标，知识涉及发动机机械结构、燃油系统、冷却系统、点火系统、充电系统、起动系统、变速器、转向系统、制动系统、车身电气系统，内容丰富、图文并茂、专业性强。全书分为 9 个单元，每个单元包括 Aims and Requirements、Know the Structure、Text A、Text B、Workshop Manual、Dialogue 六部分。

本书可作为高等职业院校汽车专业的教学用书，亦可作为汽车培训机构、汽车制造企业、汽车销售服务公司的技术培训用书。

图书在版编目（CIP）数据

汽车实用英语/吴喜骊，蒋芳编著. —北京：化学工业出版社，2021.7（2024.7 重印）
高职高专汽车类规划教材 国家技能型人才培养培训系列教材
ISBN 978-7-122-39324-1

Ⅰ.①汽… Ⅱ.①吴… ②蒋… Ⅲ.①汽车工程-英语-高等职业教育-教材 Ⅳ.①U46

中国版本图书馆 CIP 数据核字（2021）第 110570 号

责任编辑：韩庆利　　　　　　　　　　　装帧设计：史利平
责任校对：张雨彤

出版发行：化学工业出版社（北京市东城区青年湖南街 13 号　邮政编码 100011）
印　　装：北京天宇星印刷厂
787mm×1092mm　1/16　印张 9¾　字数 235 千字　2024 年 7 月北京第 1 版第 3 次印刷

购书咨询：010-64518888　　　　　　　　售后服务：010-64518899
网　　址：http://www.cip.com.cn

定　　价：34.00 元　　　　　　　　　　　　　　　　　版权所有　违者必究

随着汽车制造全球化、汽车服务国际化的不断推进，我国汽车市场新车型、新技术不断涌现，进口整车、零部件不断增加，英文原版汽车手册、维修资料、检测设备随处可见，汽车仪表、熔断器、继电器、传感器等零部件也大多采用英文来标记。汽车服务行业的变化对从业人员提出了新的挑战和更高的要求，本书的编写就是为了提高汽车专业学生和汽车服务从业人员的英文阅读水平，以适应行业发展需要。

本书以汽车专业知识和公共英语知识为基础，以训练汽车英文文献的阅读、翻译能力为目标，知识涉及汽车发动机、底盘、电气系统等，内容丰富、图文并茂、专业性强。本书可作为高等职业院校汽车专业的教学用书，亦可作为汽车培训机构、汽车制造企业、汽车销售服务公司的技术培训用书。

全书分为 9 个单元，每个单元包括 Aims and Requirements、Know the Structure、Text A、Text B、Workshop Manual、Dialogue 六部分。 Aims and Requirements 是本单元的学习目标和要求。 Know the Structure 是针对汽车总成的结构认知，帮助读者尽快熟悉零部件的英文名称。 Text A、Text B 作为单元知识的主体部分，讲解现代汽车的典型结构和原理，附有单词、词组和难句注释，课后练习包括课堂小问题、词组互译、词汇填空、缩略词表达、短句翻译。Workshop Manual 辅助读者熟悉汽车维修手册的结构、句型，涉及拆装、维修、检测、故障诊断等方面的知识。Dialogue 遴选汽车服务行业常见的对话场景，涉及汽车营销、保险、美容、维修等。每个单元中配套二维码数字资源，内容包括汽车英文注释、音频讲解。另外配套电子课件，可到 QQ 群 107141977 下载。

本书由包头职业技术学院吴喜骊（第 1～第 5 单元）、蒋芳（第 6～第 9 单元，附录 A、B）共同编写。在编写过程中，得到了内蒙古北方重型汽车股份有限公司李来平正高级工程师的大力支持，提出了许多宝贵意见和建议，在此深表谢意。

由于编者水平有限，书中不妥及疏漏之处在所难免，敬请广大读者给予批评指正。

编著者

目 录

Unit 5 — 60
Engine Charging and Starting System

Unit 6 — 75
Automobile Transmission

Unit 7 — 89
Automobile Steering System

Unit 8 — 102
Automobile Brake System

Engine Mechanical System

Aims and Requirements

- List the main components of an engine
- List the components of piston assembly
- List the types of piston ring
- Describe the function of connecting rod
- Describe the function of crankshaft
- Explain the concept of valve timing
- Translate the workshop manual
- Practice dialogues
- Cultivate students' good professional ethics
- Cultivate students' learning ability

Know the Structure

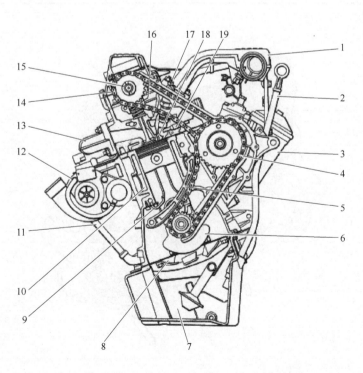

注释

Fig. 1-1　Diesel Engine

1. Charge air collector	
2. Oil dipstick	
3. Oil filter	
4. Fuel injection pump chain	
5. Tensioner rail	
6. Crankshaft	
7. Oil sump	
8. Reinforcement plate	
9. Piston cooling jet	
10. Cooling water jacket	
11. Oil return from turbocharger	
12. Turbocharger	
13. Exhaust manifold	
14. Camshaft drive chain	
15. Camshaft	
16. Hydraulic tappet	
17. Fuel injector	
18. Swirl chamber	
19. Glow plug	

注释

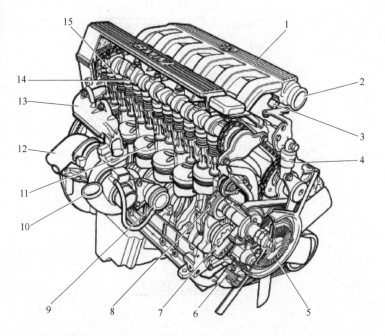

Fig. 1-2　Gasoline Engine

1. Charge air collector	
2. Connection from intercooler	
3. Intake air temperature sensor groove	
4. Hydraulic damper-tensioner roller	
5. Radiator fan	
6. Torsional vibration damper	
7. Oil pump	
8. Water pump	
9. Vacuum cell for turbocharger	
10. Turbocharger air intake	
11. Piston	
12. Exhaust pipe from turbocharger	
13. Exhaust manifold	
14. Overhead camshaft	
15. Hydraulic tappet	

Text A   Crank and Connecting Rod Mechanism

Piston Assembly

The piston is an important part of a four-stroke cycle engine. Most pistons are made from cast aluminum. The piston, through the connecting rod, transfers to the crankshaft. The force creates by the burning fuel mixture and turns the crankshaft. Some piston rings fit into grooves around the piston to seal the bottom of the combustion chamber. A piston pin fits into a round hole in the piston. The piston pin joints the piston to the connecting rod. The thick part of the piston that holds the piston is the pin boss.

The piston itself, its rings and the piston pin are together called the piston assembly.

Piston

As Fig. 1-3 shows, to withstand the heat of the combustion chamber, the piston must be strong. It also must be light, since it travels at high speeds as it moves up and down inside the cylinder. The piston is hollow. It is thick at the top where it takes the brunt of the heat and the expansion force. It is thin at the bottom, where there is less heat. The top part of the piston is the head, or crown. The thin part is the skirt. The sections between the ring grooves are called ring lands.

The piston crown may be flat, concave, domed or recessed. In diesel engine, the combustion chamber may be formed totally or in part in the piston crown, depending on the method of injection. So they use pistons with different

Fig. 1-3   Piston

shapes.

Piston Rings

As Fig. 1-4 shows，piston rings fit into ring grooves. In simplest terms，piston rings are thin，circular pieces of metal that fit into grooves in the tops of the pistons.

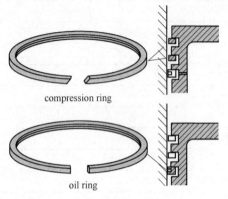

compression ring

oil ring

Fig. 1-4　Piston Rings

In modern engines，each piston has three rings. （Piston in older engines sometimes had four rings，or even five.）The ring's outside surface presses against the cylinder walls. Rings provide the needed seal between the piston and the cylinder walls. That is，only the rings contact the cylinder walls. The top two rings are to keep the gases in the cylinder and are called compression rings. The lower one prevents the oil splashed onto the cylinder bore from entering the combustion chamber，and is called an oil ring[1]. Chrome-face cast-iron compression rings are commonly used in automobile engines. The chrome face provides a very smooth，wear-resistant surface.

During the power stroke，combustion pressure on the combustion rings is very high. It causes them to untwist. Some of the high-pressure gas gets in back of the rings. This forces the ring face into full contact with the cylinder wall. The combustion pressure also holds the bottom of the ring tightly against the bottom of the ring groove. Therefore，high combustion pressure causes a tighter seal between the ring face and the cylinder wall.

Piston Pin

The piston pin holds together the piston and the connecting rod. This pin fits into the piston pin hole and into a hole in the top end of the connecting rod[2]. The top end of the connecting rod is much smaller than the end that fits on the crankshaft. This small end fits inside the bottom of the piston. The piston pin fits through one side of the piston，through the small end of the rod，and then through the other side of the piston. It holds the rod firmly in place in the center of the piston. Pins are made of high-strength steel and have a hollow center. Many pins are chrome-plated to help them wear better.

Connecting Rod

The connecting rod is made of forged high-strength steel. It transmits motion from the piston to the crankpin on the crankshaft. The connecting rod little end is connected to the piston pin. A bush made from a soft metal，such as bronze，is used for this joint. The lower end of the connecting rod fits the crankshaft journal. This is called the big end. For this big-end bearing，steel-backed lead or tin shell bearings are used[3]. These are the same as those used for the main bearings. The split of the big end is sometimes at an angle，so that it is small enough to be withdrawn through the cylinder bore[4].

Crankshaft

The crankshaft，in conjunction with the connecting rod，converts the reciprocating motion of the piston to the rotary motion needed to drive the vehicle[5]．It is usually made from carbon steel that is alloyed with a small proportion of nickel. The main bearing journals fit into the cylinder block and the big end journals align with the connecting rods. At the rear end of the crankshaft is attached the flywheel，and at the front end are the driving wheels for the timing gears，fan，cooling water pump and alternator.

Flywheel

The flywheel is made from carbon steel. It fits onto the rear of the crankshaft. As well as keeping the engine rotating between power strokes it also carries the clutch，which transmits the drive to the transmission，and has the starter ring gear around its circumference[6]． There is only one working stroke in four so a flywheel is needed to drive the crankshaft during the time that the engine is performing the non-power strokes.

New Words

groove	[gru:v]	n. 凹槽
assembly	[ə'sembli]	n. 部件，组件，集合，装配
brunt	[brʌnt]	n. 冲击，冲势
crown	[kraun]	n. 王冠，花冠，顶
concave	['kɔn'keiv]	adj. 凹的，凹入的；n. 凹，凹面
domed	[dəumd]	adj. 有穹顶的，半球形的
recess	[ri'ses]	vt. 使凹进
circular	['se:kjulə]	adj. 圆形的，循环的
chrome	[krəum]	n. 铬，铬合金
wear	[wer]	vt. 穿，戴；v. 磨损，用旧
resistant	[ri'zistənt]	adj. 抵抗的，有抵抗力的
untwist	['ʌn'twist]	v. 拆开，解开
tightly	['taitli]	adv. 紧紧地，坚固地
firmly	['fə:mli]	adv. 坚定地，稳固地
transmit	[trænz'mit]	vt. 传输，传达，传播
bush	[buʃ]	n. 衬套
bronze	[brɔnz]	n. 青铜；adj. 青铜色的
journal	['dʒə:nl]	n. 定期刊物，杂志，轴颈，枢轴
tin	[tin]	n. 锡；adj. 锡制的
shell	[ʃel]	n. 壳，外形
split	[split]	n. 裂口，裂痕；v.（使）裂开，分裂
withdraw	[wið'drɔ:]	vt. 收回，撤销；v. 撤退
forge	[fɔ:dʒ]	v. 铸造，伪造

conjunction	[kən'dʒʌŋkʃən]	n. 联合，关联，连接词
reciprocating	[ri'siprəkeitiŋ]	adj. 往复的，来回的，交替的，摆动的
carbon	['kɑːbən]	n. 碳
proportion	[prə'pɔːʃen]	n. 比例，部分
nickel	['nikl]	n. 镍
circumference	[sə'kʌmfərəns]	n. 圆周，周围

Phrases and Expressions

piston ring	活塞环
piston pin	活塞销
pin boss	销孔座
ring groove	环槽
ring land	环岸
cylinder wall	气缸壁
compression ring	压缩环
cylinder bore	气缸，缸径
oil ring	油环
high-strength steel	高强度钢
main bearing	主轴承
alloy steel	合金钢
in conjunction with	与……协力，与……联合
align with	与……结盟
timing gear	正时齿轮

Notes to the Text

[1]　The lower one prevents the oil splashed onto the cylinder bore from entering the combustion chamber, and is called an oil ring.

　　最下面的活塞环是油环，用于防止飞溅到气缸壁上的机油进入燃烧室。

音频讲解 [1]　音频讲解 [2]

[2]　This pin fits into the piston pin hole and into a hole in the top end of the connecting rod.

　　活塞销与活塞销孔及连杆小头相配合。

[3]　For this big-end bearing, steel-backed lead or tin shell bearings are used.

　　连杆轴承在钢制的轴承骨架上镀了一层铅或锡。

音频讲解 [3]　音频讲解 [4]

[4]　The split of the big end is sometimes at an angle, so that it is small enough to be withdrawn through the cylinder bore.

　　连杆大端的轴承盖切口有时做成倾斜的，这样可以使大端尺寸更小，以便从气缸中取出。

音频讲解 [5]　[5]　The crankshaft, in conjunction with the connecting rod, converts the reciprocating motion of the piston to the rotary motion needed to drive the vehicle.

曲轴通过连杆将活塞的往复运动变为旋转运动，从而驱动汽车行驶。

[6] As well as keeping the engine rotating between power strokes it also carries the clutch，which transmits the drive to the transmission，and has the starter ring gear around its circumference.

音频讲解 [6]

除了保证发动机在做功行程间转动，飞轮还带有离合器，用于将动力传递给变速器，另外在其圆周上还安装着起动齿圈。

Exercises

1. Answer the following questions according to the text

(1) What are the most pistons made from?

(2) How does the piston transfer to the crankshaft?

(3) What is the piston assembly made up of?

(4) What is the shape of piston crown?

(5) How many piston rings does each piston have in modern engine?

(6) What is the function of piston rings?

(7) Why is the split of the big end sometimes at an angle?

(8) Where is the flywheel mounted?

2. Translate the following into Chinese

(1) be made from

(2) fit into

(3) prevent from

(4) be made of

(5) such as

(6) the same as

(7) convert to

(8) at the rear end of

3. Translate the following into English

(1) 活塞环

(2) 活塞销

(3) 环槽

(4) 环岸

(5) 压缩环

(6) 油环

(7) 主轴承

(8) 合金钢

4. Fill in the blanks with the words or phrases given below，change the form where necessary

small	motion	depend on	such as
joint	seal	ring land	so that

(1) The piston pin _____ the piston to the connecting rod.

(2) The sections between the ring grooves are called _____ .

(3) In diesel engine, the combustion chamber may be formed totally or in part in the piston crown, _____ the method of injection.

(4) Rings provide the needed _____ between the piston and the cylinder walls.

(5) The top end of the connecting rod is much _____ than the end that fits on the crankshaft.

(6) It transmits _____ from the piston to the crankpin on the crankshaft.

(7) A bush made from a soft metal, _____ bronze, is used for this joint.

(8) The split of the big end is sometimes at an angle, _____ it is small enough to be withdrawn through the cylinder bore.

Text B   Valve System

Valve Timing

Inlet Valve Timing

If the inlet valve opened at TDC of the intake stroke and closed at BDC of that stroke, it would have remained open for half of a complete 360° revolution, or 180°. However, it takes some time for the valve to open to its full position. It also takes time for it to close tightly. Therefore the valve is opened before TDC (BTDC) and closed after BDC (ABDC) .

Exhaust Valve Timing

If the exhaust valve opened at BDC at the beginning of the exhaust stroke and closed at TDC at the end of the exhaust stroke, it would have a duration of 180°. But like the inlet valve, the exhaust valve needs time to reach the full-open position, it also needs time to reach the full-closed position. So the exhaust valve opens before BDC and closes after TDC.

Valve Overlap

The intake valve opens at 17° BTDC and the exhaust valve closes at 17° ATDC. Thus, for a period of 34°, both of the valves are open (17° + 17° = 34°) . This period of time is known as valve overlap. The closing of the exhaust valve laps over the opening of the intake valve. During this time, the new mixture pushes the burned gases out the exhaust valve. Valve overlap is held to a minimum on turbo-charged engines. This prevents the intake charge from being blown out the exhaust.

Valve Train

To coordinate the four-stroke cycle, a group of parts called the valve train opens and closes the valves (moves them down and up, respectively) . These valve movements must take place at exactly the right moments. The opening of each valve is controlled by a camshaft.

Overhead Camshaft Valve Train

The cam is an egg-shaped piece of metal on a shaft that rotates in coordination with the crankshaft[1] . The metal shaft, called the camshaft, typically has individual cams for each valve in the engine. As the camshaft rotates, the lobe, or high spot of the cam, pushes against parts connected to the stem of the valve. This action forces the valve to move downward. This action could open an inlet valve for an intake stroke, or open an exhaust valve for an exhaust stroke.

As the camshaft continues to rotate, the high spot moves way from the valve mechanism. As this occurs, valve springs pull the valve tightly closed against its opening, called the valve seat.

Valves in modern car engines are located in the cylinder head at the top of the engine. This is known as an overhead valve (OHV) configuration. In addition, when the camshaft is located over the cylinder head, the arrangement is known as an overhead camshaft (OHC) design. Some high-performance engines have two separate camshafts, one for each set of inlet and exhaust valves. These engines are known as dual overhead camshaft (DOHC) engines.

Push-rod Valve Train

The camshaft also can be located in the lower part of the engine, within the engine block. To transfer the motion of the cam upward to the valve, additional parts are needed.

In this arrangement, the cam lobes push against round metal cylinders called cam follower. As the lobe of the cam comes up under the cam follower, it pushes the cam follower upward (away from the camshaft). The cam follower rides against a push rod, which pushes against a rocker arm. The rocker arm pivots on a shaft through its center. As one side of the rocker arm moves up, the other side moves down, just like a seesaw. The downward-moving side of the rocker arm pushes on the valve stem to open the valve[2].

Because a push-rod valve train has additional parts, it is more difficult to run at high speeds. Push-rod engines typically run at slower speeds, consequently, produce less horsepower than overhead-camshaft designs of equal size[3].

Valve Clearance

When the engine runs in compression stroke and power stroke, the valves must close tightly on their seats to produce a gas-tight seal and thus prevent the gases escaping from the combustion chamber. If the valves do not close fully the engine will not develop full power. Also the valve heads will be liable to be burnt by the passing hot gases, and there is the likelihood of the piston crown touching an open valve, which can seriously damage the engine[4].

So that the valves can close fully some clearance is needed in the operating mechanism. This means that the operating mechanism must be able to move sufficiently far enough away from the valve to allow the valves to be fully closed against its seat by the valve spring[5]. However, if the clearance is set too great, this will cause a light metallic tapping noise.

Camshaft Drive Mechanism

Each cam must revolve once during the four-stroke cycle to open a valve. A cycle corresponds with two revolutions of the crankshaft. Therefore, the camshaft must revolve at exactly half the speed of the crankshaft. This is accomplished with a 2∶1 gear ratio. A gear connected to the camshaft has twice the number of teeth as a gear connected to the crankshaft. The gears are linked in one of three ways：

Gear Drive

The camshaft and crankshaft gears can be connected directly，or meshed. This type of operating linkage commonly is used on older six-cylinder，in-line engines.

A camshaft driven by a chain or belt turns in the same direction as the crankshaft. But a camshaft driven directly by the crankshaft gear turns in the opposite direction.

Chain Drive

On some engines，a metal chain is used to connect the crankshaft and camshaft gears. Most push-rod engines and some OHC engines have chains.

Belt Drive

A cog-type belt can be used. Such belts are made of synthetic rubber and reinforced with internal steel or fiberglass strands[6]. The belts have teeth，or slotted spaces to engage and drive teeth on gear wheels. A belt typically is used on engines with overhead-cam valve trains.

Timing belts are commonly used because they cost less than chains and operate more quietly.

New Words

lap	［læp］	vi. 重叠，围住；vt. 包围，使重叠
turbo	［'təːbəu］	n. 涡轮，增压涡轮
blow	［bləu］	v. 风吹，吹气于
coordinate	［kəu'ɔːdinit］	vt. 调整，整理
respectively	［ri'spektivli］	adv. 分别地，各个地
coordination	［kəu,ɔːdi'neiʃən］	n. 同等，调和
typically	［'tipikəli］	adv. 代表性地，作为特色地
stem	［stem］	n. 茎，干
seesaw	［'siːsɔː］	n. 秋千
consequently	［'kɔnsikwəntli］	adv. 从而，因此
liable	［'laiəbl］	adj. 易…的，有…倾向的，很有可能的
likelihood	［'laiklihud］	n. 可能，可能性
clearance	［'kliərəns］	n. 清除
sufficiently	［sə'fiʃəntli］	adv. 十分地，充分地
correspond	［kɔris'pɔnd］	vi. 符合，协调，通信，相当，相应
accomplished	［ə'kɔmpliʃt］	adj. 完成的，熟练的，多才多艺的
chain	［tʃein］	n. 链（条）
rocker	［'rɔkə］	n. 摇杆
pivot	［'pivət］	n. 枢轴；vi. 在枢轴上转动
metallic	［mi'tælik］	adj. 金属（性）的

synthetic	［sin'θetik］	adj. 合成的，人造的，综合的
fiberglass	['faibəglɑːs］	n. 玻璃纤维，玻璃丝
strand	［strænd］	n. 线，绳

Phrases and Expressions

valve timing	气门正时
inlet valve	进气门
exhaust valve	排气门
be known as	被认为是
valve overlap	气门重叠
lap over	重叠
valve mechanism	气门机构
valve seat	气门座
overhead valve	顶置气门
dual overhead camshaft	双顶置凸轮轴
cam follower	挺柱
push rod	推杆
rocker arm	摇臂
cog-type belt	齿型带
synthetic rubber	合成橡胶

Notes to the Text

[1]　The cam is an egg-shaped piece of metal on a shaft that rotates in coordination with the crankshaft.

凸轮是位于轴上的一个"蛋形"金属块，该轴由曲轴带动旋转。

音频讲解 ［1］

[2]　The downward-moving side of the rocker arm pushes on the valve stem to open the valve.

摇臂向下运动的一侧推动气门杆打开气门。

音频讲解 ［2］

[3]　Push-rod engines typically run at slower speeds，consequently，produce less horsepower than overhead-camshaft designs of equal size.

带推杆的发动机通常转速较低，因此，比同尺寸的顶置凸轮轴发动机动力要小。

音频讲解 ［3］

[4]　Also the valve heads will be liable to be burnt by the passing hot gases，and there is the likelihood of the piston crown touching an open valve，which can seriously damage the engine.

同时，气门头部容易被高温燃气烧蚀，活塞顶部也有可能撞击开启的气门，从而严重损坏发动机。

[5]　This means that the operating mechanism must be able to move sufficiently far enough away from the valve to allow the valves to be fully closed against its seat by the valve spring.

音频讲解 ［4］　　音频讲解 ［5］

音频讲解 ［6］

就是说，操纵机构与气门之间必须留有足够的距离，从而使气门在气门弹簧的作用下完全关闭。

［6］ Such belts are made of synthetic rubber and reinforced with internal steel or fiberglass strands.

齿形带由合成橡胶制成，内部由钢丝绳或玻璃纤维加固。

Exercises

1. Translate the following abbreviations into corresponding Chinese terms

（1）TDC（top dead center）

（2）BDC（bottom dead center）

（3）BTDC（before top dead center）

（4）ABDC（after bottom dead center）

（5）OHV（overhead valve）

（6）OHC（overhead camshaft）

（7）SOHC（single overhead camshaft）

（8）DOHC（dual overhead camshaft）

2. Translate the following sentences into Chinese

（1）This prevents the intake charge from being blown out the exhaust.

（2）As the camshaft rotates，the lobe，or high spot of the cam，pushes against parts connected to the stem of the valve.

（3）Valves in modern car engines are located in the cylinder head at the top of the engine.

（4）Some high-performance engines have two separate camshafts，one for each set of inlet and exhaust valves.

（5）As one side of the rocker arm moves up，the other side moves down，just like a seesaw.

（6）So that the valves can close fully some clearance is needed in the operating mechanism.

（7）On some engines，a metal chain is used to connect the crankshaft and camshaft gears.

（8）Timing belts are commonly used because they cost less than chains and operate more quietly.

Workshop Manual

Connecting Rod Bearing Noise

Possible Cause	Remedy
1. Insufficient oil supply.	1. Inspect for low oil level and low oil pressure.
2. Carbon build-up on piston.	2. Remove carbon from piston crown.
3. Bearing clearance excessive or bearing missing.	3. Measure clearance，repair as necessary.
4. Crankshaft connecting rod journal out-of-round.	4. Measure journal dimensions，repair or replace as necessary.

Continued

Possible Cause	Remedy
5. Misaligned connecting rod or cap.	5. Repair as necessary.
6. Connecting rod bolts tightened improperly.	6. Tighten bolts with specified torque.

Valve Actuating Component Noise

Possible Cause	Remedy
1. Insufficient oil supply.	1. Check for: -Low oil level. -Low oil pressure. -Wrong hydraulic tappets.
2. Rocker arms or pivots worn.	2. Replace worn rocker arms or pivots.
3. Foreign objects or chips in hydraulic tappets.	3. Clean tappets.
4. Excessive tappet leak-down.	4. Replace valve tappet.
5. Tappet face worn.	5. Replace tappet and inspect corresponding cam lobe for wear.
6. Broken or cocked valve springs.	6. Properly seat cocked springs and replace broken springs.
7. Stem-to-guide clearance excessive.	7. Measure stem-to-guide clearance, repair as required.
8. Valve bent.	8. Replace valve.
9. Loose rocker arms.	9. Check and repair as necessary.
10. Valve seat wearing excessive.	10. Regrind valve seat and valves.
11. Missing valve lock.	11. Install valve lock.
12. Excessive engine oil.	12. Correct oil level.

Dialogue

In the Auto Repair Shop

(C: Customer   T: Technician)

T: Hello, sir. Can I help you?

C: I want to have my car repaired.

T: What's wrong with your car?

C: I heard some noise from my car several days ago.

T: Oh, really? What kind of noise? Can you describe it in detail?

C: As soon as I start the engine, I can hear a ticking noise from the engine. It sounds like a loud clock.

T: I'll certainly check it out for you.

C: When can I get my car back?

T: The time depends on what the noise problem is.

C: You know, it's really inconvenient without a car. I hope I can get my car back as soon as possible.

T：I'll try my best. Please don't forget to write your name and phone number on the repairing report. I'll call you when it is done.

C：OK. Thank you!

T：Oh，please wait a minute…

C：Is there something wrong?

T：I just looked at the car you gave me. I find there's a dent in the right fender of your car.

C：Is it serious?

T：No. I just don't want you to think that I did this.

C：Don't worry. I'll make a note here on your repairing report.

T：Thank you!

Engine Fuel System

Aims and Requirements

- List five different circuits of carburetor
- Explain how an injector works
- List the sensors of engine control unit
- Describe the function of fuel delivery system
- List the components of fuel delivery system
- Translate the workshop manual
- Practice dialogues
- Cultivate students' awareness of quality and safety
- Cultivate students' learning habits of independent thinking

Know the Structure

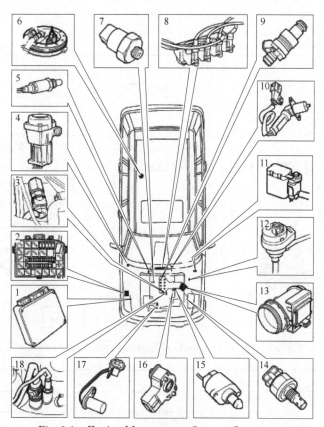

注释

Fig. 2-1   Engine Management System Component

1. Engine control module	
2. Relay box -Main relay -Ignition relay -Starter motor relay -Fuel pump relay	
3. Engine fuel temperature sensor	
4. Fuel shut-off switch	
5. Heated oxygen sensor	
6. Fuel pump	
7. Knock sensor	
8. Ignition coil	
9. Fuel injector	
10. Crankshaft position sensor	
11. Canister vent solenoid	
12. Canister purge valve	
13. Mass air flow sensor	
14. Intake air temperature sensor	
15. Idle air control valve	
16. Throttle position sensor	
17. Camshaft position sensor	
18. Engine coolant temperature sensor	

注释

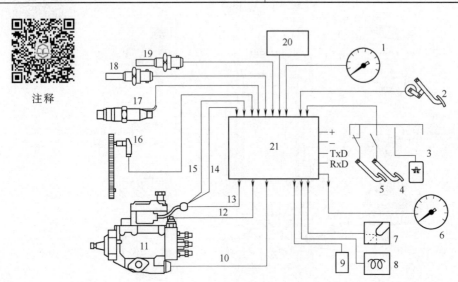

Fig. 2-2　Diesel Engine Fuel System Inputs and Outputs

1. Vehicle speed signal	
2. Throttle position sensor	
3. Cruise control selector	

Continued

4. Brake switch	
5. Clutch switch	
6. Engine speed signal	
7. Diagnostic lamp	
8. Glow plug lamp	
9. Heater time relay	
10. Injection timing device	
11. Fuel injection pump	
12. Stop solenoid	
13. Quantity servo control unit	
14. Quantity servo control potentiometer	
15. Fuel temperature sensor	
16. Crankshaft position sensor	
17. Start of injection sensor	
18. Coolant temperature sensor	
19. Intake air temperature sensor	
20. Manifold absolute pressure sensor	
21. Engine Control Module	

Text A   Fuel Injection System

In trying to keep up with emissions and fuel efficiency laws, the fuel system used in modern cars has changed a lot over the years. The 1990 Subaru Justy was the last car sold in the United States to have a carburetor, the following model year, the Justy had fuel injection. But fuel injection has been around since the 1950s, and electronic fuel injection was used widely on European cars starting around 1980. Now, all cars sold in China have fuel injection systems.

The Fall of Carburetor

For most of the existence of the internal combustion engine, the carburetor has been the device that supplied fuel to the engine. But as the automobile evolved, the carburetor got more and more complicated trying to handle all of the operating requirements. For instance, to handle some of these tasks, carburetors had five different circuits:

Main circuit — provides just enough fuel for fuel-efficient cruising.

Idle circuit — provides just enough fuel to keep the engine idling.

Accelerator pump — provides an extra burst of fuel when the accelerator pedal is first depressed, reducing hesitation before the engine speeds up.

Power enrichment circuit — provides extra fuel when the car is going up a hill or towing a trailer.

Choke — provides extra fuel when the engine is cold so that it will start.

In order to meet stricter emissions requirements, catalytic converters were introduced. Very careful control of the air-to-fuel ratio was required for the catalytic converter to be effective[1] . Oxygen sensors monitor the amount of oxygen in the exhaust, and the engine control unit (ECU) uses this information to adjust the air-to-fuel ratio in real-time. This is called closed loop control. It was not feasible to achieve this control with carburetors. There was a brief period of electrically controlled carburetors before fuel injection systems took over, but these electrical carbs were even more complicated than the purely mechanical ones.

At first, carburetors were replaced with throttle body fuel injection systems (also known as single point or central fuel injection systems) that incorporated electrically controlled fuel-injector valves into the throttle body. These were almost a bolt-in replacement for the carburetor, so the automakers didn't have to make any drastic changes to their engine designs.

Gradually, as new engines were designed, throttle body fuel injection was replaced by multi-port fuel injection (also known as port, multi-point or sequential fuel injection). These systems have a fuel injector for each cylinder, so that they spray right at the intake valve[2] . These systems provide more accurate fuel metering and quicker response.

Throttle Valve

The gas pedal in your car is connected to the throttle valve; this is the valve that regulates how much air enters the engine. So the gas pedal is really the air pedal, seeing Fig. 2-3.

Fig. 2-3　A Partially Open
Throttle Valve in Chrey Engine

When you step on the gas pedal, the throttle valve opens up more, letting in more air. The engine control unit (ECU, the computer that controls all of the electronic components on your engine) "sees" the throttle valve open and increases the fuel rate in anticipation of more air entering the engine. It is important to increase the fuel rate as soon as the throttle valve opens, otherwise, when the gas pedal is first pressed, there may be a hesitation as some air reaches the cylinders without enough fuel in it.

Sensors monitor the mass of air entering the engine, as well as the amount of oxygen in the exhaust. The ECU uses this information to fine-tune the fuel delivery so that the air-to-fuel ratio is just right.

The Injector

A fuel injector is nothing but an electronically controlled valve, seeing Fig. 2-4. It is supplied with pressurized fuel by the fuel pump in your car, and it is capable of opening and closing many times per second.

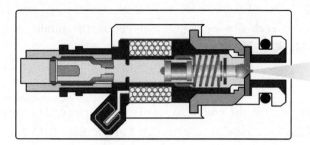

Fig. 2-4　A Fuel Injector

When the injector is energized, an electromagnet moves a plunger that opens the valve, allowing the pressurized fuel to squirt out through a tiny nozzle. The nozzle is designed to atomize the fuel-to make as fine a mist as possible so that it can burn easily[3] .

The amount of fuel supplied to the engine is determined by the amount of time the fuel injector stays open[4] . This is called the pulse width, and it is controlled by the ECU.

The injectors are mounted in the intake manifold so that they spray fuel directly at the intake valves, seeing Fig. 2-5. A pipe called the fuel rail supplies pressurized fuel to all of the injectors.

Fig. 2-5　Fuel Injectors Mounted in the Intake Manifold of the Engine

Engine Sensors

In order to provide the correct amount of fuel for every operating condition, the engine control unit (ECU) has to monitor a huge number of input sensors. Here are just a few:

Mass airflow sensor — tells the ECU the mass of air entering the engine.

Oxygen sensor — monitors the amount of oxygen in the exhaust so the ECU can determine how rich or lean the fuel mixture is and make adjustments accordingly.

Throttle position sensor — monitors the throttle valve position (which determines how much air goes into the engine) so the ECU can respond quickly to changes, increasing or decreasing the fuel rate as necessary.

Coolant temperature sensor — allows the ECU to determine when the engine has reached its proper operating temperature.

Voltage sensor — monitors the system voltage in the car so the ECU can raise the idle speed if voltage is dropping.

Manifold absolute pressure sensor — monitors the pressure of the air in the intake manifold.

Engine speed sensor — monitors engine speed, which is one of the factors used to calculate the pulse width.

There are two main types of control for multi-port systems: The fuel injectors can all open at the same time, or each one can open just before the intake valve for its cylinder opens (this is called sequential multi-port fuel injection).

Engine Controls

The algorithms that control the engine are quite complicated. The software has to allow the car to satisfy emissions requirements for 100000 miles, meet EPA fuel economy requirements. And there are dozens of other requirements to meet as well.

The engine control unit uses a formula and a large number of lookup tables to determine the pulse width for given operating conditions. The equation will be a series of many factors multiplied by each other. Many of these factors will come from lookup tables. We'll go through a simplified calculation of the fuel injector pulse width. In this example, our equation will only have three factors, whereas a real control system might have a hundred or more.

$$\text{Pulse width} = (\text{Base pulse width}) \times (\text{Factor A}) \times (\text{Factor B})$$

In order to calculate the pulse width, the ECU first looks up the base pulse width in a lookup table. Base pulse width is a function of engine speed (rpm, r/min) and load (which can be calculated from manifold absolute pressure). Let's say the engine speed is 2000rpm and load is 4. We find the number at the intersection of 2000 and 4, which is 8 milliseconds, seeing Table2-1.

In the next examples, A and B are parameters that come from sensors. A is coolant temperature and B is oxygen level. If coolant temperature equals 100 and oxygen level equals 3, the lookup tables tell us that Factor A=0. 8 and Factor B=1. 0, seeing Table2-2.

Table2-1　A Pulse Width Lookup Table

rpm	Load				
	1	2	3	4	5
1000	1	2	3	4	5
2000	2	4	6	8	10
3000	3	6	9	12	15
4000	4	8	12	16	20

Table2-2　Factor Lookup Table

A	Factor A	B	Factor B
0	1. 2	0	1. 0
25	1. 1	1	1. 0
50	1. 0	2	1. 0
75	0. 9	3	1. 0
100	0. 8	4	0. 75

So, the overall pulse width in our example equals:

$$8 \times 0. 8 \times 1. 0 = 6. 4 \text{ milliseconds}$$

From this example，you can see how the control system makes adjustments. With parameter B as the level of oxygen in the exhaust，the lookup table for B is the point at which there is（according to engine designers）too much oxygen in the exhaust，and accordingly，the ECU cuts back on the fuel.

Real control systems may have more than 100 parameters，each with its own lookup table. Some of the parameters even change over time in order to compensate for changes in the performance of engine components like the catalytic converter[5] . And depending on the engine speed，the ECU may have to do these calculations over a hundred times per second.

New Words

emission	[i'miʃən]	n.	散发，发射，喷射，排放
injection	[in'dʒekʃen]	n.	注射，喷射
existence	[ig'zistəns]	n.	存在，存在物
evolve	[i'vɔlv]	v.	（使）发展，（使）进展
requirement	[ri'kwaiəmənt]	n.	需求，要求
circuit	['sə:kit]	n.	电路，一圈
burst	[bə:st]	v.	爆裂，爆发；n. 爆发，脉冲
hesitation	[,hezi'teiʃən]	n.	犹豫，踌躇
enrichment	[in'ritʃmənt]	n.	丰富，浓缩
trailer	['treilə]	n.	追踪者，拖车
choke	[tʃəuk]	n.	窒息，阻气门
oxygen	['ɔksidʒən]	n.	氧
feasible	['fi:zəbl]	adj.	可行的，切实可行的
carb	[ka:b]	n.	化油器
throttle	['θrɔtl]	v.	扼杀
port	[pɔ:t]	n.	港口，舱门，端口
sequential	[si'kwinʃel]	adj.	连续的，相续的，有顺序的
spray	[sprei]	n.	喷雾，飞沫；vt. 喷射，喷溅
component	[kəm'pəunənt]	n.	成分；adj. 组成的，构成的
anticipation	[,æntisi'peiʃen]	n.	预期，预料
mass	[mæs]	n.	块，大多数，质量，大量
squirt	[skwə:t]	v.	喷出
nozzle	['nɔzl]	n.	管口，喷嘴
atomize	['ætəmaiz]	vt.	将…喷成雾状
accordingly	[ə'kɔ:diŋli]	adv.	因此，从而
algorithm	['ælgəriðəm]	n.	运算法则
equation	[i'kweiʃən]	n.	相等，平衡，因素，等式
multiply	['mʌltipli]	v.	繁殖，乘，增加
simplify	['simplifai]	vt.	单一化，简单化
intersection	[,intə(:)'sekʃən]	n.	十字路口，交叉点

millisecond   ['mili,sekənd]   n. 毫秒
compensate   ['kɔmpənseit]   v. 偿还，补偿，付报酬

Phrases and Expressions

fuel injection system	燃油喷射系统
main circuit	主供油系统
idle circuit	怠速系统
accelerator pump	加速泵
power enrichment circuit	加浓系统
catalytic converter	催化转换器
oxygen sensor	氧传感器
engine control unit	发动机控制单元
closed loop control	闭环控制
take over	接替
throttle body	节气门体
gas pedal	油门踏板
throttle valve	节气门阀
mass airflow sensor	空气流量传感器
throttle position sensor	节气门位置传感器
coolant temperature sensor	冷却液温度传感器
voltage sensor	电压传感器
manifold absolute pressure sensor	进气歧管压力传感器
engine speed sensor	发动机转速传感器

Notes to the Text

[1]   Very careful control of the air-to-fuel ratio was required for the catalytic converter to be effective.

为提高催化转换器的效率，必需精确控制空燃比。

音频讲解［1］

[2]   These systems have a fuel injector for each cylinder，so that they spray right at the intake valve.

多点燃油喷射系统每个气缸都有一个喷油器，在进气门附近实施喷射。

音频讲解［2］

音频讲解［3］

[3]   The nozzle is designed to atomize the fuel-to make as fine a mist as possible so that it can burn easily.

喷嘴的设计可以使燃油喷成雾状，并尽可能地细小，从而容易燃烧。

[4]   The amount of fuel supplied to the engine is determined by the amount of time the fuel injector stays open.

发动机的供油量取决于喷油器的开启时间。

音频讲解［4］

音频讲解［5］

[5]   Some of the parameters even change over time in order to compensate for changes in the performance of engine

components like the catalytic converter.

一些参数甚至随着时间在变化，用于补偿发动机附属装置性能的变化，比如催化转换器。

Exercises

1. Answer the following questions according to the text

（1）Which was the last car sold in the United States to have a carburetor?

（2）How many different circuits does the carburetor have?

（3）What is the closed loop control?

（4）Where are the injectors mounted in the multi-point fuel injection system?

（5）How many sensors are there in the fuel injection system?

（6）There are two main types of control for multi-port systems. What are they?

（7）What is the function of the mass airflow sensor?

（8）What is the function of the throttle position sensor?

2. Translate the following into Chinese

（1）try to

（2）emission law

（3）fuel efficiency

（4）for instance

（5）air-to-fuel ratio

（6）electrically controlled carburetor

（7）single point fuel injection

（8）multi-point fuel injection

3. Translate the following into English

（1）主供油系统

（2）加速泵

（3）节气门体

（4）油门踏板

（5）燃油喷射系统

（6）氧传感器

（7）冷却液温度传感器

（8）发动机转速传感器

4. Fill in the blanks with the words or phrases given below，change the form where necessary

complicated	step	come from	keep up with
a series of	nothing	so that	as soon as

（1）In trying to _____ emissions and fuel efficiency laws，the fuel system used in modern cars has changed a lot over the years.

（2）These electrical carbs were even more _____ than the purely mechanical ones.

（3）When you _____ on the gas pedal，the throttle valve opens up more，letting in more air.

（4）It is important to increase the fuel rate _____ the throttle valve opens.

(5) A fuel injector is _____ but an electronically controlled valve.

(6) The injectors are mounted in the intake manifold _____ they spray fuel directly at the intake valves.

(7) The equation will be _____ many factors multiplied by each other.

(8) Many of these factors will _____ lookup tables.

Text B　Fuel Delivery System

The function of the fuel delivery system is to store and supply fuel to either a carburetor or fuel injector, seeing Fig. 2-6. The fuel is stored in a fuel tank. A fuel pump draws the fuel from the tank through fuel lines and delivers it through a fuel filter to either a carburetor or fuel injector, then delivered to the cylinder chamber for combustion.

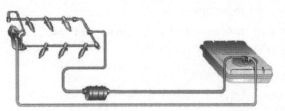

Fig. 2-6　Fuel Delivery System

Gasoline

Gasoline is a complex blend of carbon and hydrogen compounds. Additives are then added to improve performance. The two most important features of gasoline are volatility and resistance to knock (octane). Volatility is a measurement of how easily the fuel vaporizes. If the gasoline does not vaporize completely, it will not burn properly (liquid fuel will not burn).

If the gasoline vaporizes too easily the mixture will be too lean to burn properly. Since high temperature increases volatility, it is desirable to have a low volatility fuel for warm temperature and a high volatility fuel for cold weather. The blends will be different for summer and winter fuel. Vapor lock which was a persistent problem years ago, exists very rarely today. In today's cars the fuel is constantly circulating from the tank, through the system and back to the tank. The fuel does not stay still long enough to get so hot that it begins to vaporize.

Higher octane fuel requires a higher temperature to burn. As compression ratio or pressure increases so does the need for higher octane fuel[1]. Other factors that affect the octane requirements of the engine are: air-fuel ratio, ignition timing, engine temperature, and carbon build up in the cylinder. Many automobile manufacturers have installed exhaust gas recirculation systems to reduce cylinder chamber temperature. If these systems are not working properly, the car will have a tendency to knock.

Fuel Tank

Tank (Seeing Fig. 2-7) location and design are always a compromise with available space. Most automobiles have a single tank located in the rear of the vehicle. Fuel tanks today have internal baffles to prevent the fuel from sloshing back and forth. If you hear noises from the rear on acceleration and deceleration the baffles could be broken. All fuel tanks must be vented. Before 1970, fuel tanks were vented to the atmosphere, emitting hydrocarbon emissions. Since 1970 all tanks are vented through a charcoal canister, into the engine to be burned before being released to the atmosphere[2] . This is called evaporative emission control and will be discussed further in the emission control section. Federal law requires that all 1976 and newer cars have vehicle rollover protection devices to prevent fuel spills.

Fig. 2-7   Fuel Tank

Fuel Lines

Steel lines and flexible hoses carry the fuel from the tank to the engine. When servicing or replacing the steel lines, copper or aluminum must never be used. Steel lines must be replaced with steel. When replacing flexible rubber hoses, proper hose must be used. Ordinary rubber such as used in vacuum or water hose will soften and deteriorate. Be careful to route all hoses away from the exhaust system.

Fuel Pump

Two types of fuel pumps are used in automobiles: mechanical and electric. All fuel injected cars today use electric fuel pumps, while most carbureted cars use mechanical fuel pumps. Mechanical fuel pumps are diaphragm pumps, mounted on the engine and operated by an eccentric cam usually on the camshaft. A rocker arm attached to the eccentric moves up and down flexing the diaphragm and pumping the fuel to the engine. Because electric pumps depend on an eccentric for operation, they can be located anywhere on the vehicle. In fact they work best when located near the fuel tank.

Many cars today, locate the fuel pump inside the fuel tank. While mechanical pumps operate on pressures of 4~6psi (pounds per square inch), electric pumps can operate on pressures of 30~40psi. Current is supplied to the pump immediately when the key is turned. This allows for constant pressure on the system for immediate starting. Electric fuel pumps can be either low pressure or high pressure. These pumps look identical, so be careful when replacing a fuel pump that the proper one is used[3] .

Fig. 2-8   Fuel Filter

Fuel Filter

The fuel filter is the key to a properly functioning fuel delivery system, seeing Fig. 2-8. This is truer with fuel injection than with carbureted cars. Fuel injectors are more susceptible to damage from dirt because of their close tolerances, but also fuel injection cars use electric fuel pumps. When the filter clogs, the electric fuel pump works so hard to push past the filter that it burns itself up[4] . Most cars use two filters，one inside the gas tank and one in a line to the fuel injectors or carburetor. Unless some severe and unusual condition occurs to cause a large amount of dirt to enter the gas tank，it is only necessary to replace the filter in the line.

New Words

blend	［blend］	*vt.* 混合；*n.* 混合（物）
hydrogen	［'haidrəudʒən］	*n.* 氢
compound	［'kɔmpaund］	*n.* 混合物，化合物
additive	［'æditiv］	*adj.* 附加的，添加的；*n.* 添加剂
volatility	［ˌvɔlə'tiliti］	*n.* 挥发性
resistance	［ri'zistəns］	*n.* 反抗，抵抗，阻力，电阻
persistent	［pə'sistənt］	*adj.* 持久稳固的
constantly	［'kɔnstəntli］	*adv.* 不变地，经常地
octane	［'ɔktein］	*n.* 辛烷
compromise	［'kɔmprəmaiz］	*n.* 妥协，折衷；*v.* 妥协，折衷
baffle	［'bæfl］	*vt.* 困惑，阻碍，为难
slosh	［slɔʃ］	*n.* 泥泞，溅泼声；*v.* 溅，泼
charcoal	［'tʃɑːkəul］	*n.* 木炭
canister	［'kænistə］	*n.* 小罐，筒
rollover	［'rəulˌəuvə］	*n.* 翻滚
spill	［spil］	*n.* 溢出（量），溅出（量）；*vt.* 使溢出，使散落
flexible	［'fleksəbl］	*adj.* 柔韧性，柔软的，能变形的
deteriorate	［di'tiəriəreit］	*v.* （使）恶化
route	［ruːt］	*n.* 路线，路程，通道；*v.* 发送
eccentric	［ik'sentrik］	*adj.* 古怪的
susceptible	［sə'septəbl］	*adj.* 易受影响的，易感动的，容许……的
clog	［klɔg］	*n.* 木底鞋，障碍；*v.* 障碍，阻塞

Phrases and Expressions

carbon and hydrogen compound	碳氢化合物
vapor lock	气阻
compression ratio	压缩比
exhaust gas recirculation system	废气再循环系统
fuel tank	燃油箱
charcoal canister	炭罐
evaporative emission control	燃油蒸发控制
such as	比如
fuel pump	燃油泵
diaphragm pump	膜片泵

depend on	依靠，依赖
in fact	事实上
fuel filter	燃油滤清器
because of	由于

Notes to the Text

［1］　As compression ratio or pressure increases so does the need for higher octane fuel.

由于压缩比和气缸压力的增加，汽油的辛烷值要求也越高。

音频讲解 ［1］

［2］　Since 1970 all tanks are vented through a charcoal canister，into the engine to be burned before being released to the atmosphere.

从 1970 年起，所有汽油箱都通过活性炭罐进行通风，并且在释放到大气之前进入发动机被燃烧掉。

音频讲解 ［2］

［3］　These pumps look identical，so be careful when replacing a fuel pump that the proper one is used.

这些油泵看上去很相似，因此在更换时，要注意使用正确的油泵。

［4］　When the filter clogs，the electric fuel pump works so hard to push past the filter that it burns itself up.

当滤清器阻塞时，电动燃油泵会因负荷增大而烧毁。

音频讲解 ［3］　　音频讲解 ［4］

Exercises

1. Translate the following abbreviations into corresponding Chinese terms

（1）ECM（engine control module）

（2）KS（knock Sensor）

（3）CKP（crankshaft position sensor）

（4）IAT（intake air temperature sensor）

（5）MAF（mass air flow sensor）

（6）TP（throttle position sensor）

（7）CMP（camshaft position sensor）

（8）EFT（engine fuel temperature sensor）

2. Translate the following sentences into Chinese

（1）The function of the fuel delivery system is to store and supply fuel to either a carburetor or fuel injector.

（2）If the gasoline does not vaporize completely，it will not burn properly.

（3）Many automobile manufacturers have installed exhaust gas recirculation systems to reduce cylinder chamber temperature.

（4）Federal law requires that all 1976 and newer cars have vehicle rollover protection devices to prevent fuel spills.

（5）Be careful to route all hoses away from the exhaust system.

（6）All fuel injected cars today use electric fuel pumps，while most carbureted cars use mechanical fuel pumps.

（7）Because electric pumps depend on an eccentric for operation，they can be located anywhere on the vehicle.

（8）Unless some severe and unusual condition occurs to cause a large amount of dirt to enter the gas tank，it is only necessary to replace the filter in the line.

Workshop Manual

Crankshaft Position Sensor

The crankshaft position sensor is the most important sensor on the engine. It is located in the left hand side of the flywheel housing and uses a different thickness of spacer for manual and automatic gearboxes. The signal it produces informs the ECM：

— The engine is turning.

— How fast the engine is turning.

— Which stage the engine is at in the cycle.

As there is no default strategy，failure of the CKP sensor will result in the engine failing to start. The fault is indicated by illumination of the malfunction indicator light (MIL) on North American specification vehicles.

The output signal from the CKP sensor is obtained from the magnetic path being made and broken as the reluctor ring teeth pass the sensor tip. The reluctor ring has 35 teeth and one missing tooth spaced at $10°$ intervals. The missing tooth is positioned at $20°$ after TDC.

Fault codes：

P0335 — crankshaft sensor circuit fault-no signal.

P0336 — crankshaft sensor generating poor quality signal.

Throttle Position Sensor

The throttle position sensor is mounted on the throttle body in line with the throttle plate shaft. The sensor is a variable resistor，the signal from which ($0 \sim 5V$) informs the ECM of the actual position of the throttle disc and the rate of change of throttle position. This information is used by the ECM for regulation of acceleration enrichment fuelling. Sensor failure will adversely affect the acceleration performance. The closed throttle voltage is continuously monitored and updated when engine conditions indicate that the throttle is closed.

The GEMS ECM performs a throttle potentiometer range check by cross checking with the measured air flow. If the two values do not correlate and fuelling feedback indicates that fuelling and therefore airflow is correct，the potentiometer is assumed to have failed. In the event that a fault is detected，GEMS supplies a default value dependent on air flow.

The throttle angle is also supplied to the gearbox ECM，the loss of this signal will result in poor gear change quality and loss of kickdown.

Warning: If the throttle potentiometer is changed, it is necessary to reset the closed throttle voltage.

Fault codes:

P0121 — throttle potentiometer signal inconsistent with MAF, IACV, air temperature and engine rpm.

P0122 — throttle potentiometer circuit low input.

P0123 — throttle potentiometer circuit high input.

Dialogue

At the Garage

(C: Customer   T: Technician)

T: What's wrong with your car, sir?

C: I can't start the engine. It doesn't warm up.

T: Let me check it. The alternator fails to generate electricity. It must be replaced by a new one.

C: The light and the radio don't work, too.

T: I'm sorry to hear that. Oh, your engine doesn't produce enough power to turn the wheels and make the electric system distribute electricity to the spark plugs. No wonder you can't turn on the light and the radio.

C: How about the fuel system?

T: This system works well.

C: How about the speedometer and the other parts?

T: The needle is loose. The steering wheel can't move smoothly, and the gear shift···

C: It's 6: 10 now. I hope it can be repaired in half an hour, can't it?

T: I'm sorry. Maybe you can take a taxi now and get your car tomorrow.

C: Ok, thanks a lot. Bye.

T: Bye.

Engine Cooling System

Aims and Requirements

- Describe the task of cooling system
- Explain how a cooling system works
- List the types of cooling system
- Describe the circulation of cooling system
- List the components of cooling system
- Translate the workshop manual
- Practice dialogues
- Cultivate students' awareness of environmental protection
- Cultivate students' ability to analyze and solve problems

Know the Structure

注释

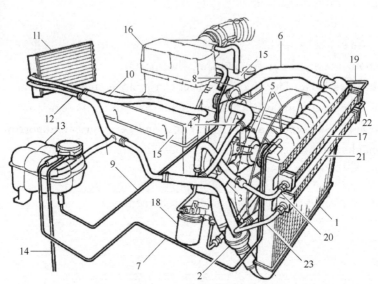

Fig. 3-1　Cooling System

1. Radiator	
2. Thermostat housing	
3. Radiator bottom hose	

续表

4. Bypass hose	
5. Fan and water pump	
6. Radiator top hose	
7. Radiator bleed pipe	
8. Plenum chamber feed pipe	
9. Plenum chamber bleed pipe	
10. Heater feed hose	
11. Heater matrix	
12. Heater return hose	
13. Expansion tank	
14. Overflow/Breather pipe	
15. Cylinder banks	
16. Plenum chamber	
17. Engine oil cooler	
18. Engine oil filter	
19. Feed pipe, engine oil cooler	
20. Return pipe, engine oil cooler	
21. Gearbox oil cooler	
22. Feed pipe, gearbox oil cooler	
23. Return pipe, gearbox oil cooler	

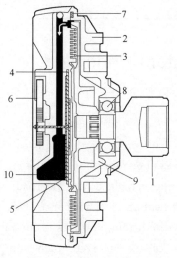

注释

Fig. 3-2   Viscous Unit

1. Input (drive) member	
2. Output (driven) member	
3. Running clearance	
4. Pump plate	
5. Valve (closed)	

6. Sensing mechanism（bi-metal coil）	
7. Fluid seal	
8. Bearing，input member	
9. Fluid chamber	
10. Fluid reservoir	

注释

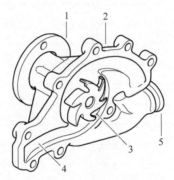

Fig. 3-3　Coolant Pump

1. Pulley flange	
2. Body	
3. Impeller	
4. Gallery	
5. Inlet connection	

Text A　Cooling System Principle

Cooling System Task

A typical 4 cylinder vehicle cruising along the highway at around 50 miles per hour，will produce 4000 controlled explosions per minute inside the engine as the spark plugs ignite the fuel in each cylinder to propel the vehicle down the road[1] . Obviously，these explosions produce an enormous amount of heat and，if not controlled，will destroy an engine in a matter of minutes. Controlling these high temperatures is the job of the cooling system.

The modern cooling system has not changed much from the cooling systems in the model T back in the 1920's. It has become infinitely more reliable and efficient at doing its job，but the basic cooling system still consists of liquid coolant being circulated through the engine，then out to the radiator to be cooled by the air stream coming through the front grill of the vehicle.

Today's cooling system must maintain the engine at a constant temperature whether the outside air temperature is 110 degrees Fahrenheit or 10 below zero. If the engine temperature is too low，fuel economy will suffer and emissions will rise. If the temperature is allowed to get too hot for too long, the engine will self destruct.

How Does a Cooling System Work

Actually, there are two types of cooling systems found on motor vehicles: liquid cooled and air cooled. Air cooled engines are found on a few older cars, like the original Volkswagen Beetle, the Chevrolet Corvair and a few others. Many modern motorcycles still use air cooling, but for the most part, automobiles and trucks use liquid cooled systems.

The cooling system is made up of the passages inside the engine block and heads, a water pump to circulate the coolant, a thermostat to control the temperature of the coolant, a radiator to cool the coolant, a radiator cap to control the pressure in the system, and some plumbing consisting of interconnecting hoses to transfer the coolant from the engine to radiator and also to the car's heater system where hot coolant is used to warm up the vehicle's interior on a cold day, seeing Fig. 3-4.

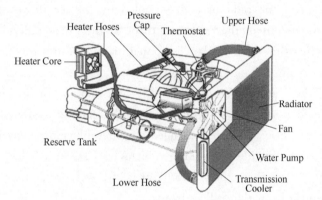

Fig. 3-4　Liquid Cooling System in BYD Engine

A cooling system works by sending a liquid coolant through passages in the engine block and heads. As the coolant flows through these passages, it picks up heat from the engine. The heated fluid then makes its way through a rubber hose to the radiator in the front of the car. As it flows through the thin tubes in the radiator, the hot liquid is cooled by the air stream entering the engine compartment from the grill in front of the car. Once the fluid is cooled, it returns to the engine to absorb more heat. The water pump has the job of keeping the fluid moving through this system of plumbing and hidden passages.

A thermostat is placed between the engine and the radiator to make sure that the coolant stays above a certain preset temperature. If the coolant temperature falls below this temperature, the thermostat blocks the coolant flow to the radiator, forcing the fluid instead through a bypass directly back to the engine. The coolant will continue to circulate like this until it reaches the design temperature, at which point, the thermostat will open a valve and allow the coolant back through the radiator[2] .

In order to prevent the coolant from boiling, the cooling system is designed to be pressurized. Under pressure, the boiling point of the coolant is raised considerably. However, too much pressure will cause hoses and other parts to burst, so a system is needed to relieve pressure if it exceeds a certain point. The job of maintaining the pressure in the cooling system belongs to the radiator cap. The cap is designed to release pressure if it reaches the specified upper limit that the system was designed to handle. Prior to the 70s, the cap would release this extra pressure to the pavement. Since then, a system was added to capture any released fluid and store it temporarily in a reserve tank. This fluid would then return to the cooling system after the engine cooled down. This is what is called a closed cooling system.

Circulation

The coolant follows a path that takes it from the water pump, through passages inside the engine block where it collects the heat produced by the cylinders[3] . It then flows up to the cylinder head where it collects more heat from the combustion chambers. It then flows out past the thermostat (if the thermostat is opened to allow the fluid to pass), through the upper radiator hose and into the radiator. The coolant flows through the thin flattened tubes that make up the core of the radiator and is cooled by the air flowed through the radiator. From there, it flows out of the radiator, through the lower radiator hose and back to the water pump. By this time, the coolant is cooled off and ready to collect more heat from the engine.

The capacity of the system is designed for the type and size of the engine and the work load that it is expected to undergo[4] . Obviously, the cooling system for a larger, more powerful V8 engine in a heavy vehicle will need considerably more capacity than a compact car with a small 4 cylinder engine. On a large vehicle, the radiator is larger with many more tubes for the coolant to flow through. The radiator is also wider and taller to capture more air flow entering the vehicle from the grill in front.

Antifreeze

The coolant that courses through the engine and associated plumbing must be able to withstand temperatures well below zero without freezing[5] . It must also be able to handle engine temperatures in excess of 250 degrees without boiling. A tall order for any fluid, but that is not all. The fluid must also contain rust inhibiters and a lubricant.

The coolant in today's vehicles is a mixture of ethylene glycol (antifreeze) and water. The recommended ratio is fifty-fifty, in other words, one part antifreeze and one part water. This is the minimum recommended for use in automobile engines. Less antifreeze and the boiling point would be too low. In certain climates where the temperatures can go well below zero, it is permissible to have as much as 75% antifreeze and 25% water, but no more than that. Pure antifreeze will not work properly and can cause a boil over.

Antifreeze is poisonous and should be kept away from people and animals. Ethylene Glycol, if ingested, can cause acute renal failure and death.

New Words

infinitely	['infinitli]	*adv.* 无限地，无穷地

circulate	['sə:kjuleit]	v. （使）流通，（使）运行，（使）循环
grill	[gril]	n. 烤架，铁格子，格栅
maintain	[men'tein]	vt. 维持，维修
destruct	[dis'trʌkt]	vi. 破坏
passage	['pæsidʒ]	n. 通过，经过，通道
coolant	['ku:lənt]	n. 冷冻剂，冷却液
thermostat	['θə:məstæt]	n. 节温器，温度调节装置
radiator	['reidieitə]	n. 散热器，水箱
plumbing	['plʌmiŋ]	n. 管道，导管
interconnect	[,intə(:)kə'nekt]	vt. 使互相连接
preset	['pri:'set]	vt. 事先调整
relieve	[ri'li:v]	vt. 减轻，解除，援救
pavement	['peivmənt]	n. 人行道，公路
reserve	[ri'zə:v]	n. 储备（物），储藏量；vt. 储备，保存
flatten	['flætn]	vt. 使平，变平
undergo	[ʌndə'gəu]	vt. 经历，遭受，忍受
compact	['kɔmpækt]	adj. 紧凑的，紧密的，简洁的
inhibiter	[in'hibitə]	n. 抑制剂，抑制者
recommend	[rekə'mend]	vt. 推荐，介绍
antifreeze	['ænti'fri:z]	n. 防冻剂
poisonous	['pɔiznəs]	adj. 有毒的
ingest	[in'dʒest]	vt. 摄取，咽下，吸收

Phrases and Expressions

in a matter of	大约，大概
cooling system	冷却系统
liquid cooled	水冷
air cooled	风冷
water pump	水泵
radiator cap	散热器盖
engine compartment	发动机舱
in excess of	超过
ethylene glycol	乙烯乙二醇
keep away from	远离

Notes to the Text

[1]　A typical 4 cylinder vehicle cruising along the highway at around 50 miles per hour，will produce 4000 controlled explosions per minute inside the engine as the spark plugs ignite the fuel in each cylinder to propel the vehicle down the road.

音频讲解 [1]

音频讲解 [2]

音频讲解 [3]

音频讲解 [4]

音频讲解 [5]

一辆四缸发动机汽车沿着公路以每小时 50 英里的速度行驶，随着火花塞的不断点火，每分钟内发动机将产生 4000 次爆发燃烧。

[2] The coolant will continue to circulate like this until it reaches the design temperature，at which point，the thermostat will open a valve and allow the coolant back through the radiator.

冷却液不断地在发动机水套中循环，当水温升高到设计温度时，节温器打开阀门使冷却水流回散热器。

[3] The coolant follows a path that takes it from the water pump，through passages inside the engine block where it collects the heat produced by the cylinders.

冷却液从水泵中流出，经过发动机水套时，吸收来自气缸的热量。

[4] The capacity of the system is designed for the type and size of the engine and the work load that it is expected to undergo.

设计冷却系统的散热能力时，要适应发动机的型式和尺寸，以及它所承受的工作负荷。

[5] The coolant that courses through the engine and associated plumbing must be able to withstand temperatures well below zero without freezing.

流经发动机及其管道的冷却液应能承受零度以下的低温，而不会结冰。

Exercises

1. Answer the following questions according to the text

(1) What is the cooling system task?

(2) What kind of cooling system is used on most modern cars?

(3) Can you list the basic components of the cooling system?

(4) What keep the fluid circulating in the cooling system?

(5) Why is the cooling system designed to be pressurized?

(6) How does the radiator cap maintain the pressure in the cooling system?

(7) Why does the coolant contain antifreeze?

(8) What is the coolant made from in today's vehicles?

2. Translate the following into Chinese

(1) be made up of

(2) consist of

(3) pick up

(4) makes one's way to

(5) make sure

(6) belong to

(7) by this time

(8) no more than

3. Translate the following into English

(1) 冷却系统

（2）水冷

（3）风冷

（4）水泵

（5）散热器盖

（6）发动机舱

（7）膨胀水箱

（8）风扇皮带

4. Fill in the blanks with the words or phrases given below, change the form where necessary

prior to	in a matter of	by this time	belong to
make sure	keep away from	in excess of	in order to

（1）Obviously, these explosions produce an enormous amount of heat and, if not controlled, will destroy an engine _____ minutes.

（2）A thermostat is placed between the engine and the radiator to _____ that the coolant stays above a certain preset temperature.

（3）_____ prevent the coolant from boiling, the cooling system is designed to be pressurized.

（4）The job of maintaining the pressure in the cooling system _____ the radiator cap.

（5）_____ , the coolant is cooled off and ready to collect more heat from the engine.

（6）_____ the 70s, the cap would release this extra pressure to the pavement.

（7）It must also be able to handle engine temperatures _____ 250 degrees without boiling.

（8）Antifreeze is poisonous and should be _____ people and animals.

Text B　The Components of Cooling System

Radiator

Seeing Fig. 3-5, the radiator core is usually made of flattened aluminum tubes with aluminum strips that zigzag between the tubes. These fins transfer the heat in the tubes into the air stream to be carried away from the vehicle. On each end of the radiator core is a tank, usually made of plastic that covers the ends of the radiator. On most modern radiators, the tubes run horizontally with the plastic tank on either side. On other cars, the tubes run vertically with the tank on the top and bottom. On older vehicles, the core was made of copper and the tanks were brass. The new aluminum-plastic system is much more efficient, not to mention cheaper to produce[1] . On radiators with plastic tanks, there are gaskets between the aluminum core and the plastic tanks to seal the system and keep the fluid from leaking out. On older copper and brass radiators, the tanks were brazed (a form of welding) in order to seal the radiator.

The tanks, whether plastic or brass, each have a large hose connection, one mounted towards the top of the radiator to let the coolant in, the other mounted at the bottom of the

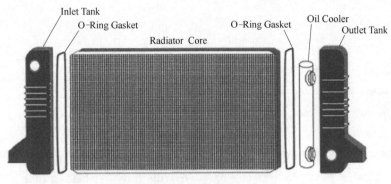

Fig. 3-5   Radiator

radiator on the other tank to let the coolant back out. On the top of the radiator is an additional opening that is capped by the radiator cap.

Radiator Fan

Mounted on the back of the radiator on the side closest to the engine is one or two electric fans inside a housing that is designed to direct the air flow[2] . These fans are there to keep the air flow going through the radiator while the vehicle is going slow or is stopped with the engine running. If these fans stopped working, every time you came to a stop, the engine temperature would begin rising. On older systems, the fan was connected to the front of the water pump and would spin whenever the engine was running because it was driven by a fan belt instead of an electric motor.

The electric fans are controlled by the vehicle's computer. A temperature sensor monitors engine temperature and sends this information to the computer. The computer determines if the fan should be turned on and actuates the fan relay if additional air flow through the radiator is necessary.

Pressure Cap and Reserve Tank

As coolant gets hot, it expands. Since the cooling system is sealed, this expansion causes an increase in pressure in the cooling system. The radiator pressure cap is a simple device that will maintain pressure in the cooling system up to a certain point. If the pressure builds up higher than the set pressure point, there is a spring loaded valve, opened to release the pressure[3] .

When the cooling system pressure reaches the point where the cap needs to release this excess pressure, a small amount of coolant is bled off. It could happen during stop and go traffic on an extremely hot day, or if the cooling system is malfunctioning. If it does release pressure under these conditions, there is a system in place to capture the released coolant and store it in a plastic tank that is usually not pressurized. Since there is now less coolant in the system, as the engine cools down a partial vacuum is formed. The radiator cap on these closed systems has a secondary valve to allow the vacuum in the cooling system to draw the coolant back into the radiator from the reserve tank.

Water Pump

See Fig. 3-6, a water pump is a simple device that will keep the coolant moving as long as the engine is running. It is usually mounted on the front of the engine and turns whenever the engine is running. The water pump is driven by the engine through the fan belt or the timing belt.

The water pump is made up of a housing, usually made of cast iron or cast aluminum and an impeller mounted on a spinning shaft with a pulley attached to the shaft on the outside of the pump body. A seal keeps fluid from leaking out of the pump housing past the spinning shaft. The impeller uses centrifugal force

Fig. 3-6　Water Pump

to draw the coolant in from the lower radiator hose and send it under pressure into the engine block. There is a gasket to seal the water pump to the engine block and prevent the flowing coolant from leaking out where the pump is attached to the block.

Thermostat

The thermostat is simply a valve that measures the temperature of the coolant and, if it

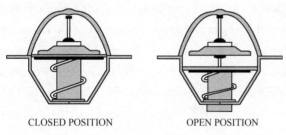

CLOSED POSITION　　OPEN POSITION

Fig. 3-7　Thermostat

is hot enough, opens to allow the coolant to flow through the radiator, seeing Fig. 3-7. If the coolant is not hot enough, the flow to the radiator is blocked and fluid is directed to a bypass system that allows the coolant to return directly back to the engine[4] . Because flow to the radiator is blocked, the engine will reach operating temperature sooner and, on a cold day, will allow the heater to begin supplying hot air to the interior more quickly.

The heart of a thermostat is a sealed copper cup that contains wax and a metal pellet. As the thermostat heats up, the hot wax expands, pushing a piston against spring pressure to open the valve and allow coolant to circulate.

The thermostat is usually located in the front, top part of the engine in a water outlet housing that also serves as the connection point for the upper radiator hose[5] . The thermostat housing attaches to the engine, usually with two bolts and a gasket to seal it against leaks. The gasket is usually made of a heavy paper or a rubber "O" ring is used.

Bypass System

This is a passage that allows the coolant to bypass the radiator and return directly back to the engine. Some engines use a rubber hose, or a fixed steel tube. In other engines, there is a cast in passage built into the water pump or front housing. In any case, when the thermostat is closed, coolant is directed to this bypass and channeled back to the water pump, which sends the coolant back into the engine without being cooled by the radiator.

Heater Core

The hot coolant is also used to provide heat to the interior of the vehicle when needed. This is a simple system that includes a heater core, which looks like a small version of a radiator, connected to the cooling system with a pair of rubber hoses, seeing Fig. 3-8. One hose brings hot coolant from the water pump to the heater core and the other hose returns the coolant to the top of the engine. There is usually a heater control valve in one of the hoses to block the flow of coolant into the heater core when maximum air conditioning is called for[6] .

Fig. 3-8　Heater Core

A fan, called a blower, draws air through the heater core and directs it through the heater ducts to the interior of the car.

Hoses

There are several rubber hoses that make up the plumbing to connect the components of the cooling system. The main hoses are called the upper and lower radiator hoses. These two hoses are approximately 2 inches in diameter and direct coolant between the engine and the radiator. Two additional hoses, called heater hoses, supply hot coolant from the engine to the heater core. These hoses are approximately 1 inch in diameter. A fifth hose, called the bypass hose, is used to circulate the coolant through the engine, bypassing the radiator, when the thermostat is closed.

These hoses are designed to withstand the pressure inside the cooling system. Because of this, they are subject to wear and tear and eventually may require replacing as part of routine maintenance. If the rubber is beginning to look dry and cracked, or becomes soft and spongy, it is time to replace them. The main radiator hoses are usually molded to a shape that is designed to rout the hose around obstacles.

There is a small rubber hose that runs from the radiator neck to the reserve bottle. This allows coolant that is released by the pressure cap to be sent to the reserve tank. This rubber hose is about a quarter inch in diameter and is normally not part of the pressurized system. Once the engine is cool, the coolant is drawn back to the radiator by the same hose.

New Words

zigzag	['zigzæg]	v. 成 Z 字形，曲折前进
brass	[brɑːs]	n. 黄铜，黄铜制品
braze	[breiz]	vt. 铜焊

monitor	['mɔnitə]	*vt.* 监控	
wax	[wæks]	*n.* 蜡，蜡状物	
pellet	['pelit]	*n.* 小球	
bypass	['baipɑːs]	*n.* 旁路；*vt.* 设旁路，迂回	
version	['vəːʃən]	*n.* 形式，种类	
blower	['bləuə]	*n.* 送风机，吹风机	
duct	[dʌkt]	*n.* 管，输送管	
approximately	[əprɔksɪ'mətlɪ]	*adv.* 近似地，大约	
tear	[tiə]	*vi.* 撕破，被撕破	
routine	[ruː'tiːn]	*n.* 常规，日常事务，程序	
spongy	['spʌndʒi]	*adj.* 像海绵的，柔软的	
mold	[məuld]	*n.* 模子，铸型；*vt.* 浇铸，塑造	

Phrases and Expressions

keep from	防止……
bleed off	放出，排出
reserve tank	膨胀水箱
fan belt	风扇皮带
timing belt	正时皮带
centrifugal force	离心力
heater core	加热器
be subject to	遭受……
call for	要求，请求

Notes to the Text

[1]　The new aluminum-plastic system is much more efficient, not to mention cheaper to produce.

新型的铝塑系统效率更高，而且制造成本低廉。

音频讲解 [1]

[2]　Mounted on the back of the radiator on the side closest to the engine is one or two electric fans inside a housing that is designed to direct the air flow.

在散热器的后面靠近发动机一侧安装着一个或两个电子风扇，风扇位于一个用于引导空气流动的壳体内。

音频讲解 [2]

[3]　If the pressure builds up higher than the set pressure point, there is a spring loaded valve, opened to release the pressure.

如果压力超出设定值，弹簧阀门就会打开释放压力。

音频讲解 [3]　音频讲解 [4]

[4]　If the coolant is not hot enough, the flow to the radiator is blocked and fluid is directed to a bypass system that allows the coolant to return directly back to the engine.

如果冷却液温度不高，通往散热器的通道就会被堵塞，冷却液直接经过一个旁通道流回发动机。

[5] The thermostat is usually located in the front，top part of the engine in a water outlet housing that also serves as the connection point for the upper radiator hose.

节温器通常安装在发动机前端、顶部的一个出水口处，它同时连接着散热器的上水管。

[6] There is usually a heater control valve in one of the hoses to block the flow of coolant into the heater core when maximum air conditioning is called for.

在其中一根软管上安装有加热器控制阀，当空调开到最大时，用于切断流向加热器的冷却液。

Exercises

1. Translate the following abbreviations into corresponding Chinese terms

(1) VECS (vehicle engine cooling system)

(2) WCLD (water cooled)

(3) CCCS (computer controlled cooling system)

(4) CTS (coolant temperature switch)

(5) ECL (engine coolant level)

(6) ECT (engine coolant temperature)

(7) LLC (long life coolant)

(8) CF (cooling fan)

2. Translate the following sentences into Chinese

(1) On most modern radiators，the tubes run horizontally with the plastic tank on either side.

(2) On the top of the radiator is an additional opening that is capped by the radiator cap.

(3) The computer determines if the fan should be turned on and actuates the fan relay if additional air flow through the radiator is necessary.

(4) The radiator pressure cap is a simple device that will maintain pressure in the cooling system up to a certain point.

(5) A water pump is a simple device that will keep the coolant moving as long as the engine is running.

(6) There is a gasket to seal the water pump to the engine block and prevent the flowing coolant from leaking out where the pump is attached to the block.

(7) This is a passage that allows the coolant to bypass the radiator and return directly back to the engine.

(8) These hoses are designed to withstand the pressure inside the cooling system.

Workshop Manual

Engine Overheating

Possible Cause	Remedy
1. Engine coolant low.	1. Allow engine to cool. Top up expansion tank to correct level, with engine running at idle. Check cooling system for leaks and rectify, if necessary.
2. Loose drive belt.	2. Check/renew drive belt tensioner or renew drive belt.
3. Coolant in radiator frozen.	3. Slowly thaw and drain cooling system.
4. Air flow through radiator restricted or blocked.	4. Apply air pressure to engine side of radiator to clear obstruction.
5. External leaks from water pump, engine gaskets, thermostat housing or pipe.	5. Check for visual causes and rectify.
6. Viscous fan not operating correctly or inoperative.	6. Renew viscous fan unit.
7. Thermostat seized in closed position.	7. Check radiator bottom hose. If cold, a faulty thermostat is confirmed. Renew thermostat assembly.
8. Air in cooling system.	8. Check coolant level. Run engine at fast idle with expansion tank cap off. Top up coolant level with engine at idle and refit expansion tank cap.
9. Temperature gauge or sender unit giving inaccurate readings.	9. Substitute parts and compare new readings.
10. Coolant leakage across cylinder head gasket.	10. Carry out cylinder pressure test to determine if pressure is leaking into cooling system, causing loss of coolant. Renew cylinder head gasket.
11. Engine oil contamination of cooling system due to leaking.	11. Renew cylinder head gasket.
12. Coolant contamination of lubrication system.	12. Renew inlet manifold or front cover gaskets.

Engine Runs Cold

Possible Cause	Remedy
1. Thermostat seized in open or partially open position.	1. Remove thermostat housing and check operation of thermostat. Renew, if necessary.
2. Temperature gauge or sender unit giving inaccurate readings.	2. Substitute parts and compare new readings.
3. Viscous fan not operating correctly.	3. Renew viscous fan unit.
4. Air conditioning condenser fans operating continuously.	4. See Air conditioning fault diagnosis.

Dialogue

Selecting and Buying a Car

(C: Customer   S: Salesman)

S：Good morning，sir. Can I help you?

C：I'd like to buy a car. Recommend one for me?

S：Is it for personal or business use?

C：It's for personal use. Would you tell me some more details?

S：With pleasure. Why not go to the showroom? I'll show you around. We have many models displayed there.

C：Great! Let's go!

······

S：Look! All our models are here. I think there is one type that suits you.

C：I hope so.

S：Sir，how about this one? This car has excellent safety features，like the dual air bags and ABS brakes. Compared with the old types，this type is improved in exterior design and tint. It offers high level of comfort and eye-catching styling，and some optional equipments are also offered.

C：It looks really nice! But it's a little more than I could pay.

S：Oh，how about that yellow one? It has the characteristics of small volume，stable property，safety and reliability，low fuel consumption，long life in service. Besides，the price is moderate.

C：It's quite good. But I prefer the white color.

S：The white ones of this type are out of stock. Can you wait?

C：OK. if not waiting for a long time.

S：It would not keep you waiting for more than one week. Please fill in this form，and I'll call you as soon as possible.

C：All right! Thank you for you help.

S：My pleasure.

Engine Ignition System

Aims and Requirements

- Describe the tasks of ignition system
- List the types of ignition system
- Explain how the mechanical ignition system works
- Describe the distributorless ignition system
- List the components of the mechanical ignition system
- Translate the workshop manual
- Practice dialogues
- Establish awareness of civilized production and safe operation
- Cultivate students' information processing ability

Know the Structure

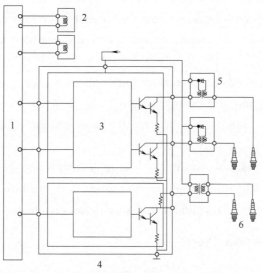

注释

Fig. 4-1   Ignition System Circuit Diagram

1. PCM	
2. Crankshaft position sensor	
3. Driver	
4. Igniter	
5. Ignition coil	
6. Spark plug	

注释

Fig. 4-2   Spark Plug

1. Nut	
2. Insulator	
3. Up-washer	
4. Housing	
5. Gasket	
6. Ground electrode	
7. Central electrode	

Text A   Ignition System Principle

The purpose of the ignition system is to create a spark that will ignite the fuel-air mixture in the cylinder of an engine. It must do this at exactly the right instant and do it at the rate of up to several thousand times per minute for each cylinder in the engine. If the timing of that spark is off by a small fraction of a second, the engine will run poorly or not run at all.

The ignition system sends an extremely high voltage to the spark plug in each cylinder when the piston is at the top of its compression stroke. The tip of each spark plug contains a gap that the voltage must jump across in order to reach ground. That is where the spark occurs.

The voltage that is available to the spark plug is somewhere between 20, 000 volts and 50, 000 volts or better. The job of the ignition system is to produce that high voltage from a 12-volt source and get it to each cylinder in a specific order, at exactly the right time.

Ignition System Tasks and Types

The ignition system has two tasks to perform. First, it must create a voltage high enough to arc across the gap of a spark plug, thus creating a spark strong enough to ignite the air-fuel mixture for combustion. Second, it must control the timing of the spark so it occurs at the exact right time and send it to the correct cylinder.

The ignition system is divided into two sections, the primary circuit and the secondary circuit. The low voltage primary circuit operates at battery voltage (12 to 14. 5 volts) and is responsible for generating the signal to fire the spark plug at the exact right time and sending that signal to the ignition coil[1] . The ignition coil is the component that converts the 12 volts signal into the high 20, 000 volts charge. Once the voltage is stepped up, it goes to the secondary circuit which then directs the charge to the correct spark plug at the right time.

Currently, there are three distinct types of ignition systems. The mechanical ignition system was used prior to 1975. It was mechanical and electrical and used no electronics. The electronic ignition system started finding its way to production vehicles during the early 70s and became popular when better control and improved reliability became important with the advent of emission controls. Finally, the distributorless ignition system became available in the mid 80s. This system was always computer controlled and contained no moving parts, so reliability was greatly improved. Most of these systems required no maintenance except replacing the spark plugs at intervals from 60, 000 to over 100, 000 miles.

The Mechanical Ignition System

The distributor is the nerve center of the mechanical ignition system and has two tasks to perform. First, it is responsible for triggering the ignition coil to generate a spark at the precise instant that it is required (which varies depending how fast the engine is turning and how much load it is under) . Second, the distributor is responsible for directing that spark to the proper cylinder, seeing Fig. 4-3.

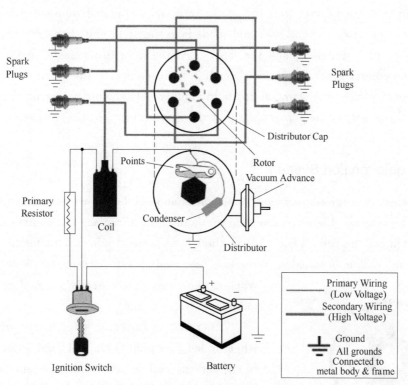

Fig. 4-3 The Mechanical Ignition System

The circuit that powers the ignition system is simple and straight forward. When you insert the key in the ignition switch and turn the key to the run position, current is sent from the battery through a wire directly to the positive (＋) side of the ignition coil. Inside the coil is a series of copper windings that loop around the coil over a hundred times before exiting out the negative (－) side of the coil. From there, a wire takes this current over to the distributor and is connected to a special on-off switch, called the points. When the points are closed, this current goes directly to ground. When current flows from the ignition switch, through the windings in the coil, then to ground, it builds a strong magnetic field inside the coil.

The points are made up of a fixed contact point that is fastened to a plate inside the distributor, and a movable contact point mounted on the end of a spring loaded arm. The movable point rides on a 4, 6, or 8 lobe cam (depending on the number of cylinders in the engine) that is mounted on a rotating shaft inside the distributor. This distributor cam rotates in time with the engine, making one complete revolution for every two revolutions of the engine. As it rotates, the cam pushes the points open and closed. Every time the points open, the flow of current is interrupted through the coil, thereby collapsing the magnetic field and releasing a high voltage surge through the secondary coil windings. This voltage surge goes out the top of the coil and through the high-tension coil wire.

The coil wire goes from the coil directly to the center of the distributor cap. Under the cap is a rotor that is mounted on top of the rotating shaft. The rotor has a metal strip on the top that is in constant contact with the center terminal of the distributor cap. It receives the high voltage surge from the coil wire and sends it to the other end of the rotor which rotates past each spark plug terminal inside the cap[2] . As the rotor turns on the shaft, it sends the voltage to the correct spark plug wire, which in turn sends it to the spark plug. The voltage enters the spark plug at the terminal at the top and travels down the core until it reaches the tip. It then jumps across the gap at the tip of the spark plug, creating a spark suitable to ignite the air-fuel mixture inside that cylinder.

The Electronic Ignition System

In the electronic ignition system, the points and condenser were replaced by electronics. On these systems, there were several methods used to replace the points and condenser in order to trigger the coil to fire. One method used a metal wheel with teeth, usually one for each cylinder. This is called an armature, seeing Fig. 4-4. A magnetic pickup coil senses when a tooth passes and sends a signal to the control module to fire the coil[3] .

Other systems used an electric eye with a shutter wheel to send a signal to the electronics that it was time to trigger the coil to fire. These systems still need to have the initial timing adjusted by rotating the distributor housing.

The advantage of this system, aside from the fact that it is maintenance free, is that the control module

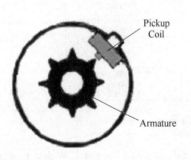

Pickup Coil

Armature

Fig. 4-4　Ignition Signal Sensor

can handle much higher primary voltage than the mechanical points. Voltage can even be stepped up before sending it to the coil, so the coil can create a much hotter spark, on the order of 50000 volts instead of 20000 volts that is common with the mechanical system[4]. These systems only have a single wire from the ignition switch to the coil since a primary resistor is no longer needed.

On some vehicles, this control module was mounted inside the distributor where the points used to be mounted. On other designs, the control module was mounted outside the distributor with external wiring to connect it to the pickup coil. On many General Motors engines, the control module was inside the distributor and the coil was mounted on top of the distributor for a one-piece unitized ignition system. GM called it high energy ignition or HEI for short.

The higher voltage that these systems provided allow the use of a much wider gap on the spark plugs for a longer, fatter spark. These larger sparks also allow a leaner mixture for better fuel economy and still insure a smooth running engine.

The early electronic systems had limited or no computing power, so timing still had to be set manually and there was still a centrifugal and vacuum advance built into the distributor.

On some of the later systems, the inside of the distributor is empty and all triggering is performed by a sensor that watches a notched wheel connected to either the crankshaft or the camshaft[5]. These devices are called crankshaft position sensor or camshaft position sensor. In these systems, the job of the distributor is solely to distribute the spark to the correct cylinder through the distributor cap and rotor. The computer handles the timing and any timing advance necessary for the smooth running of the engine.

The Distributorless Ignition System

Newer automobiles have evolved from a mechanical system (distributor) to a completely solid state electronic system with no moving parts. These systems are completely controlled by the on-board computer. In place of the distributor, there are multiple coils that each serves one or two spark plugs. A typical 6-cylinder engine has 3 coils that are mounted together in a coil pack. A spark plug wire comes out of each side of the individual coil and goes to the appropriate spark plug. The coil fires both spark plugs at the same time. One spark plug fires on the compression stroke igniting the air-fuel mixture to produce power, while the other spark plug fires on the exhaust stroke and does nothing. On some vehicles, there is an individual coil for each cylinder mounted directly on top of the spark plug. This design completely eliminates the high-tension spark plug wires for even better reliability. Most of these systems use spark plugs that are designed to last over 100, 000 miles, which cuts down on maintenance costs.

New Words

specific   [spi'sifik]   n. 细节；adj. 精确的，明确的，特殊的

responsible	[ris'pɔnsəbl]	adj.有责任的，可靠的，可依赖的
distinct	[dis'tiŋkt]	adj.清楚的，明显的，独特的
reliability	[ri,laiə'biliti]	n.可靠性
advent	['ædvənt]	n.出现，到来
nerve	[nə:v]	n.神经，胆量，勇气
trigger	['trigə]	vt.引发，引起，触发
precise	[pri'sais]	adj.精确的，准确的；n.精确
copper	['kɔpə]	n.铜
strip	[strip]	vt.剥，剥去；n.条，带
suitable	['sju:təbl]	adj.适当的，相配的
condenser	[kən'densə]	n.电容器
armature	['ɑ:mətjuə]	n.电枢
shutter	['ʃʌtə]	n.关闭者，百叶窗
initial	[i'niʃəl]	adj.最初的，词首的，初始的
resistor	[ri'zistə]	n.电阻器
unitized	['ju:nitaizd]	adj.组成的，合成的，成套的
notched	[nɔtʃt]	adj.有凹口的，有锯齿状的
appropriate	[ə'prəupriit]	adj.适当的
eliminate	[i'limineit]	vt.排除，消除；v.除去

Phrases and Expressions

spark plug	火花塞
primary circuit	初级电路
secondary circuit	次级电路
ignition coil	点火线圈
mechanical ignition system	机械点火系统
electronic ignition system	电子点火系统
distributorless ignition system	无分电器点火系统
ignition switch	点火开关
magnetic field	磁场
fixed contact point	固定触点
movable contact point	移动触点
secondary coil	次级线圈
high-tension wire	高压线
distributor cap	分电器盖
pickup coil	传感线圈
distributor housing	分电器壳体
aside from	除了，除……以外
control module	控制模块
step up	走近，逐步增加，提升，提高

on the order of	属于……一类的，与……相似的
instead of	代替，而不是……
high energy ignition（HEI）	高能点火
centrifugal advance	离心提前
vacuum advance	真空提前
crankshaft position sensor	曲轴位置传感器
camshaft position sensor	凸轮轴位置传感器
distributor rotor	分火头
at the same time	同时

Notes to the Text

[1]　The low voltage primary circuit operates at battery voltage（12 to 14.5 volts）and is responsible for generating the signal to fire the spark plug at the exact right time and sending that signal to the ignition coil.

低压初级电路由蓄电池供电（12～14.5V），担负着在恰当的时刻产生点火信号并将信号送给点火线圈的任务。

音频讲解［1］

[2]　It receives the high voltage surge from the coil wire and sends it to the other end of the rotor which rotates past each spark plug terminal inside the cap.

分火头将高压脉冲从中央高压线送至分电器旁电极。

音频讲解［2］

[3]　A magnetic pickup coil senses when a tooth passes and sends a signal to the control module to fire the coil.

当凸齿经过时，磁感应线圈产生感应信号，并将信号送给控制模块用于触发点火线圈。

音频讲解［3］

[4]　Voltage can even be stepped up before sending it to the coil，so the coil can create a much hotter spark，on the order of 50，000 volts instead of 20，000 volts that is common with the mechanical system.

由于提高了点火线圈的初级电压，因此点火线圈能够产生高能火花，可以达到 50000 伏，而不是机械点火系统的 20000 伏。

音频讲解［4］

[5]　On some of the later systems，the inside of the distributor is empty and all triggering is performed by a sensor that watches a notched wheel connected to either the crankshaft or the camshaft.

在近期的系统中，分电器内部是空的，点火触发信号由一个传感器产生，该传感器用于感应连接在曲轴或凸轮轴上的转子的脉冲信号。

音频讲解［5］

Exercises

1. Answer the following questions according to the text

（1）What is the purpose of the ignition system?

（2）The ignition system has two tasks to perform，what are they?

（3）The ignition system is divided into two sections，what are they?

（4）What are three distinct types of ignition systems?

（5）Can you list the basic components of mechanical ignition system?

（6）What is the function of point?

（7）What are the advantages of electronic ignition system?

（8）What is the high energy ignition?

2. Translate the following into Chinese

（1）at the right instant

（2）divide into

（3）prior to

（4）find one's way to

（5）no longer

（6）be made up of

（7）aside from

（8）cut down

3. Translate the following into English

（1）初级电路

（2）次级电路

（3）机械点火系统

（4）电子点火系统

（5）无分电器点火系统

（6）点火开关

（7）高压导线

（8）高能点火

4. Fill in the blanks with the words or phrases given below，change the form where necessary

in turn	no longer	aside from	be responsible for
prior to	divide into	jump across	in place of

（1）The tip of each spark plug contains a gap that the voltage must_____in order to reach ground.

（2）The ignition system is_____two sections，the primary circuit and the secondary circuit.

（3）The mechanical ignition system was used_____1975.

（4）Second，the distributor_____directing that spark to the proper cylinder.

（5）As the rotor turns on the shaft，it sends the voltage to the correct spark plug wire，which_____sends it to the spark plug.

（6）The advantage of this system，_____the fact that it is maintenance free，is that the control module can handle much higher primary voltage than the mechanical points.

（7）These systems only have a single wire from the ignition switch to the coil since a primary resistor is_____needed.

（8）_____the distributor，there are multiple coils that each serves one or two spark plugs.

Text B   The Components of Ignition System

Ignition Switch

There are two separate circuits that go from the ignition switch to the coil. One circuit runs through a resistor in order to step down the voltage about 15% in order to protect the points from premature wear. The other circuit sends full battery voltage to the coil. The only time this circuit is used is during cranking. Since the starter draws a considerable amount of current to crank the engine, additional voltage is needed to power the coil. So when the key is turned to the spring-loaded start position, full battery voltage is used. As soon as the engine is running, the driver releases the key to the run position which directs current through the primary resistor to the coil.

On some vehicles, the primary resistor is mounted on the firewall and is easy to replace if it fails. On other vehicles, the primary resistor is a special resistor wire and is bundled in the wiring harness with other wires, making it more difficult to replace, but also more durable[1] .

Distributor

When you remove the distributor cap from the top of the distributor, you will see the points and condenser. The condenser is a simple capacitor that can store a small amount of current. When the points begin to open, the current flowing through the points looks for an alternative path to ground. If the condenser were not there, it would try to jump across the gap of the points as they begin to open. If this were allowed to happen, the points would quickly burn up and you would hear heavy static on the car radio. To prevent this, the condenser acts like a path to ground. It really is not, but by the time the condenser is saturated, the points are too far apart for the small amount of voltage to jump across the wide point gap[2] . Since the arcing across the opening points is eliminated, the points last longer and there is no static on the radio from point arcing.

The points require periodic adjustments. This is because there is a rubbing block on the points that is in contact with the cam and this rubbing block wears out over time changing the point gap. There are two ways that the points can be measured to see if they need an adjustment. One way is by measuring the gap between the open points when the rubbing block is on the high point of the cam. The other way is by measuring the dwell electrically. The dwell is the amount, in degrees of cam rotation, that the points stay closed.

On some vehicles, points are adjusted with the engine off and the distributor cap removed. A mechanic will loosen the fixed point and move it slightly, then retighten it in the correct position using a feeler gauge to measure the gap. On other vehicles, there is a window in the distributor where a mechanic can insert a tool and adjust the points using a dwell meter while the engine is running. Measuring dwell is much more accurate than setting the points with a feeler gauge. Points have a life expectancy of about 10，000 miles at which time they have to be replaced.

Ignition Coil

The ignition coil is nothing more that an electrical transformer. It contains both primary and secondary winding circuits. The coil primary winding contains 100 to 150 turns of heavy copper wire. This wire must be insulated so that the voltage does not jump from loop to loop，shorting it out. If this happened，it could not create the primary magnetic field that is required. The primary circuit wire goes into the coil through the positive terminal，loops around the primary windings，then exits through the negative terminal.

The coil secondary winding circuit contains 15，000 to 30，000 turns of fine copper wire，which also must be insulated from each other. The secondary windings sit inside the loops of the primary windings. To further increase the coils magnetic field the windings are wrapped around a soft iron core. To withstand the heat of the current flow，the coil is filled with oil which helps keep it cool.

The ignition coil is the heart of the ignition system. As current flows through the coil a strong magnetic field is built up. When the current is shut off，the collapse of this magnetic field to the secondary windings induces a high voltage which is released through the large center terminal[3]. This voltage is then directed to the spark plugs through the distributor.

Ignition Timing

The timing is set by loosening a hold-down screw and rotating the body of the distributor. Since the spark is triggered at the exact instant that the points begin to open，rotating the distributor body (which the points are mounted on) will change the relationship between the position of the points and the position of the distributor cam，which is on the shaft that is geared to the engine rotation[4].

While setting the initial，or base timing is important，for an engine to run properly，the timing needs to change depending on the speed of the engine and the load that it is under. If we can move the plate that the points are mounted on，or we could change the position of the distributor cam in relation to the gear that drives it，we can alter the timing dynamically to suit the needs of the engine.

There are two mechanisms that allow the timing to change：centrifugal advance and vacuum advance.

Centrifugal advance changes the timing in relation to the speed of the engine. It uses a pair of weights that are connected to the spinning distributor shaft. These weights are hinged on one side to the lower part of the shaft and connected by a linkage to the upper shaft where the distributor cam is. The weights are held close to the shaft be a pair of springs. As the shaft spins faster，the weights are pulled out by centrifugal force against the spring pressure. The faster the shaft spins，the more they are pulled out. When the weights move out，it changes the alignment between the lower and upper shaft，causing the timing to advance.

Vacuum advance works by changing the position of the points in relationship to the distributor body. Vacuum advance uses a vacuum diaphragm connected to a link that can move the plate that the points are mounted on[5] . By sending engine vacuum to the vacuum advance diaphragm，timing is advanced. On cars，the vacuum that is used is port vacuum，which is just above the throttle plate. With this setup，there is no vacuum present at the vacuum advance diaphragm while the throttle is closed. When the throttle is opened，vacuum is sent to the vacuum advance，advancing the timing.

Both Vacuum and Centrifugal advance systems worked together to extract the maximum efficiency from the engine. If either system were not functioning properly，both performance and fuel economy would suffer. Once computer controls were able to directly control the engine's timing，vacuum and centrifugal advance mechanisms were no longer necessary and were eliminated.

Ignition Wires

These cables are designed to handle 20，000 to more than 50，000 volts. The job of the spark plug wires is to get that enormous power to the spark plug without leaking out. Spark plug wires have to endure the heat of a running engine as well as the extreme changes in the weather. In order to do their job，spark plug wires are fairly thick，with most of that thickness devoted to insulation with a very thin conductor running down the center.

Spark plug wires go from the distributor cap to the spark plugs in a very specific order. This is called the "firing order" . Each spark plug must only fire at the end of the compression stroke. Each cylinder has a compression stroke at a different time，so it is important that the wires are installed correctly. If the wires are installed incorrectly，the engine may backfire，or not run on all cylinders.

Spark Plugs

The ignition system must provide sufficient voltage to jump the gap at the tip of the spark plug and do it at the exact right time，reliably on the order of thousands of times per minute for each spark plug in the engine.

Most spark plugs contain a resistor to suppress radio interference. The gap on a spark plug is also important and must be set before the spark plug is installed in the engine. If the gap is too wide，there may not be enough voltage to jump the gap，causing a misfire. If the gap is too small，the spark may be inadequate to ignite a lean air-fuel mixture，also causing a misfire.

New Words

premature	[ˌpreməˈtjuə]	adj. 未成熟的，太早的，早熟的
considerable	[kənˈsidərəbl]	adj. 相当大的，值得考虑的，相当可观的
durable	[ˈdjuərəbl]	adj. 持久的，耐用的
capacitor	[kəˈpæsitə]	n. 电容器

alternative	[ɔːˈltəːnətiv]	*adj*. 选择性的，二者择一的
static	[ˈstætik]	*adj*. 静态的；*n*. 静电干扰
saturated	[ˈsætʃəreitid]	*adj*. 渗透的，饱和的，深颜色的
rub	[rʌb]	*v*. 擦，摩擦
expectancy	[ikˈspektənsi]	*n*. 期待，期望
transformer	[trænsˈfɔːmə]	*n*. 变压器
insulate	[ˈinsjuleit]	*vt*. 使绝缘，隔离
wrap	[ræp]	*vt*. 包装，卷，缠绕
collapse	[kəˈlæps]	*n*. 倒塌，崩溃；*vi*. 倒塌，崩溃，瓦解
induce	[inˈdjuːs]	*vt*. 促使，导致，引起
hinge	[hindʒ]	*vt*. 装铰链
extract	[iksˈtrækt]	*vt*. 拔出，榨取，吸取
suffer	[ˈsʌfə]	*vt*. 遭受，经历；*vi*. 受痛苦，受损害
enormous	[iˈnɔːməs]	*adj*. 巨大的，庞大的
endure	[inˈdjuə]	*v*. 耐久，忍耐
suppress	[səˈpres]	*vt*. 镇压，抑制，使止住
inadequate	[inˈædikwit]	*adj*. 不充分的，不适当的
misfire	[ˈmisˈfaiə]	*v*. 失火

Phrases and Expressions

feeler gauge	塞尺
nothing more that	不过，不外乎
primary winding	初级绕组
secondary winding	次级绕组
distributor cam	分电器凸轮
in relation to	关于，涉及，与……相比
distributor shaft	分电器轴
throttle plate	节气门
as well as	也，又
devote to	专心于，致力于

Notes to the Text

音频讲解 [1]

[1]　On other vehicles, the primary resistor is a special resistor wire and is bundled in the wiring harness with other wires, making it more difficult to replace, but also more durable.

在有些车上，初级电阻是一根特殊的电阻线，与其它线路一起绑成线束，更换起来比较困难，但更加可靠。

音频讲解 [2]

[2]　It really is not, but by the time the condenser is saturated, the points are too far apart for the small amount of voltage to jump across the wide point gap.

电容器并不是真正地对地导通，但是当电容器饱和时，触点已经远离，两端的感应电压已经不能击穿触点间隙了。

音频讲解〔3〕

〔3〕　When the current is shut off, the collapse of this magnetic field to the secondary windings induces a high voltage which is released through the large center terminal.

当电流切断时，磁场的迅速消失，在次级绕组中感应出一个高压脉冲，并从点火线圈的中央电极输出。

音频讲解〔4〕

〔4〕　Since the spark is triggered at the exact instant that the points begin to open, rotating the distributor body (which the points are mounted on) will change the relationship between the position of the points and the position of the distributor cam, which is on the shaft that is geared to the engine rotation.

由于火花是在触点打开的时刻触发的，因此转动分电器壳体（触点安装在上面）就会改变触点与分电器凸轮的相对位置，凸轮安装在随发动机旋转的分电器轴上。

音频讲解〔5〕

〔5〕　Vacuum advance uses a vacuum diaphragm connected to a link that can move the plate that the points are mounted on.

真空提前机构中的真空膜片通过接杆连到触点的固定底板上。

Exercises

1. Translate the following abbreviations into corresponding Chinese terms

（1）ICM（ignition control module）

（2）DLI（distributorless ignition）

（3）DI（distributor ignition）

（4）IT（ignition timing）

（5）CCI（computer controlled ignition）

（6）PW（primary winding）

（7）SI（spark ignition）

（8）HEI（high energy ignition）

2. Translate the following sentences into Chinese

（1）There are two separate circuits that go from the ignition switch to the coil.

（2）Points have a life expectancy of about 10，000 miles at which time they have to be replaced.

（3）The ignition coil is nothing more that an electrical transformer.

（4）The coil secondary winding circuit contains 15，000 to 30，000 turns of fine copper wire, which also must be insulated from each other.

（5）To withstand the heat of the current flow, the coil is filled with oil which helps keep it cool.

（6）Centrifugal advance changes the timing in relation to the speed of the engine.

（7）Vacuum advance works by changing the position of the points in relationship to the distributor body.

(8) Each cylinder has a compression stroke at a different time, so it is important that the wires are installed correctly.

Workshop Manual

Inspection of Spark Plug

(1) Disconnect the spark plug cable from the spark plug.

(2) Using a plug wrench, remove all the spark plugs from the cylinder head.

(3) Check the spark plugs for the following: broken insulator, worn electrode, carbon deposits, damaged or broken gasket, burnt condition of porcelain insulator at the spark gap.

(4) Check the spark plug gap using a wire gap gage and adjust if necessary (standard value: 1.0~1.1mm).

(5) Tighten spark plug to specified torque (standard value: 20~30Nm).

Checking Ignition Timing

Despite the speed that an engine turns, it is possible for you to be able to check the ignition timing of an engine using an ignition timing light. Timing lights are typically strobe lights. They work by being connected to the battery directly and then having an induction coil clamped around one of the spark plug leads—normally the first or last cylinder in the engine depending on the manufacturer. When the engine fires the spark plug for that cylinder, the inductive loop detects the current in the wire and flashes the strobe light once. So if the engine is running at 1100rpm, the strobe will flash 550 times a minute. Somewhere on the front of the engine there will be a notch near one of the timing belt pulleys and stamped into the metal next to it will be timing marks in degrees. On the pulley itself there will be a bump, recess or white-painted blob. When you point the strobe light down towards the timing belt pulley, each time it fires, the white blob on the pulley should be at the same position in its rotation. The mark on the pulley will line up with one of the degree marks stamped on the engine, so for example if the white dot always aligns with the $10°$ mark, it means your engine is firing at 10 degrees before TDC. When you rev the engine, the timing will change so the mark will move closer or further away from the TDC mark depending on how fast the engine is spinning.

Dialogue

At the Exhibition

(C: Customer S: Salesman)

C: Good morning.

S: Good morning.

C: Nice to meet you.

S: Take a seat, please. What can I do for you?

C: I'd like to buy a large quantity of vans if your price is competitive enough.

S: We can easy supply you with that.

C: Now I'd like to have a look at the samples on exhibition.

S: This way, please.

(A few minutes later)

S: Here are the samples. The vans are available in all models.

C: Mm. They look very beautiful.

S: They are well known for their fine quality and attractive appearance.

C: The quality seems all right, but the price are too high.

S: I don't believe you could buy vans of the similar quality and fashionable design at such a price elsewhere.

C: If we could come to terms on price, I may order in quality at once.

S: Our manager is coming here soon. We can make a further discussion.

C: Ok. Thank you very much.

S: My pleasure.

Engine Charging and Starting System

Aims and Requirements

- Describe the charging system task
- List the main components of alternator
- Explain how a voltage regulator works
- Describe the function of charging system warning lamp
- List the components of starting system
- Describe five switch positions of an ignition switch
- Translate the workshop manual
- Practice dialogues
- Strictly follow the automobile maintenance industry standards
- Cultivate students' communication ability

Know the Structure

注释

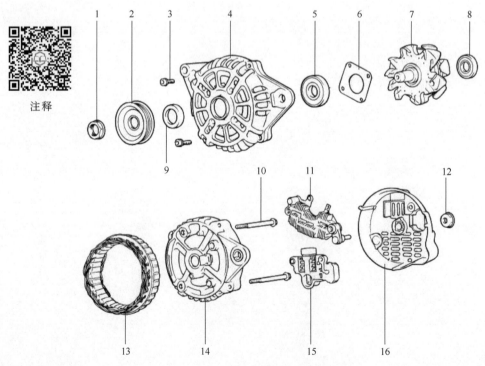

Fig. 5-1 Generator

1. Hex nut	
2. Pulley	
3. Screw	
4. Front housing	
5. Front bearing	
6. Retainer	
7. Rotor assembly	
8. Rear bearing	
9. Spacer	
10. Bolt	
11. Rectifier	
12. B terminal	
13. Stator assembly	
14. Rear housing	
15. Regulator assembly	
16. Cover	

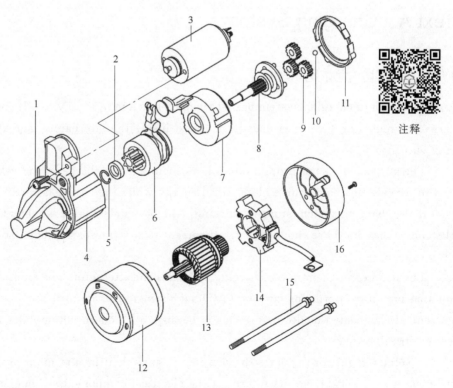

注释

Fig. 5-2　Starter

1. Screw	
2. Snap ring	
3. Solenoid	
4. Front bracket	
5. Stop ring	
6. Overrun clutch	
7. Ring gear	
8. Sun gear	
9. Planetary gear	
10. Ball	
11. Packing	
12. Yoke assembly	
13. Armature	
14. Brush holder	
15. Screw	
16. Rear bracket	

Text A Charging System

What Is a Charging System

The modern charging system hasn't changed much in over 40 years. It consists of the alternator, regulator (which is usually mounted inside the alternator) and the interconnecting wiring.

The purpose of the charging system is to maintain the charge in the vehicle's battery, and to provide the main source of electrical energy while the engine is running.

If the charging system stopped working, the battery's charge would soon be depleted, the engine may not have enough electrical current to fire the spark plugs, so the engine will stop running.

The main component in the charging system is the alternator. The alternator is a generator that produces alternating current (AC). This current is immediately converted to direct current (DC) inside the alternator. This is because all modern automobiles have a 12-volt, DC electrical system.

A voltage regulator regulates the charging voltage that the alternator produces, keeping it between 13.5 and 14.5 volts to protect the electrical components throughout the vehicle.

There is also a system to warn the driver if something is not right with the charging system. This could be a dash mounted voltmeter, an ammeter, or more commonly, a warning lamp. If this warning lamp lights up while the engine is running, it means that there is a problem in the charging system, usually an alternator that has stopped working. The most common cause is a broken alternator drive belt.

The alternator is driven by a belt which is powered by the engine. This belt goes around a pulley connected to the front of the engine's crankshaft and is usually responsible for driving a number of other components including the water pump, power steering pump and air conditioning compressor[1] . On some engines, there is more than one belt and the task of driving these components is divided between them. These belts are usually referred to as: fan belt, alternator belt, power steering belt, A/C belt, etc. More common on late model engines, one belt, called a serpentine belt will snake around the front of the engine and drive all the components by itself.

On engines with separate belts for each component, the belts will require periodic adjustments to maintain the proper belt tension. On engines that use a serpentine belt, there is usually a spring loaded belt tensioner that maintains the tension of the belt, so no periodic adjustments are required. A serpentine belt is designed to last around 30, 000 miles.

Alternator

The alternator uses the principle of electromagnetism to produce current. The way this works is simple. If you take a strong magnet and pass it across a wire, that wire will generate a small voltage. Take that same wire and loop it many times, than if you pass the same magnet across the bundle of loops, you create a more sizable voltage in that wire.

There are two main components that make up an alternator. They are the rotor and the stator, seeing Fig. 5-3 and Fig. 5-4. The rotor is connected directly to the alternator pulley. The drive belt spins the pulley, which in turn spins the rotor. The stator is mounted to the body of the alternator and remains stationary. There is just enough room in the center of the stator for the rotor to fit and be able to spin without making any contact.

Fig. 5-3　Rotor

The stator contains 3 sets of wires that have many loops each and are evenly distributed to form a three-phase system. On some systems, the wires are connected to each other at one end and are connected to a rectifier assembly on the other end. On other systems, the wires are connected to each other end to end, and at each of the three connection points, there is also a connection to the rectifier.

The rotor contains the powerful magnet that passes close to the many wire loops that make up the stator[2] . The magnets in the rotor are actually electro magnets, not permanent magnets. This is

Fig. 5-4　Stator　done so that we can control how much voltage the alternator produces by regulating the amount of current that creates the magnetic field in the rotor[3] . In this way, we can control the output of the alternator to suit our needs, and protect the circuits in the automobile from excessive voltage.

When we spin the rotor inside the stator and apply current to the rotor through a pair of brushes that make constant contact with two slip rings on the rotor shaft, this causes the rotor to become magnetized. The alternating north and south pole magnets spin past the three sets of wire loops in the stator and produce a constantly reversing voltage in the three wires. In other words, we are producing alternating current in the stator.

Now, we have to convert this alternating current to direct current, this is done by using a series of 6 diodes that are mounted in a rectifier assembly. A diode allows current to flow only in one direction. If voltage tries to flow in the other direction, it is blocked. The six diodes are arranged so that all the voltage coming from the alternator is aligned in one direction thereby converting AC current into DC current.

Current to generate the magnetic field in the rotor comes from the ignition switch and passes through the voltage regulator. Since the rotor is spinning, we need a way to connect this current from the regulator to the spinning rotor. This is accomplished by wires connected to two spring loaded brushes which rub against two slip rings on the rotor shaft[4] . The voltage regulator monitors the voltage coming out of the alternator and, when it reaches a threshold of about 14.5 volts, the regulator reduces the current in the rotor to weaken the magnetic field. When the voltage drops below this threshold, the current to the rotor is increased.

Voltage Regulator

The voltage regulator can be mounted inside or outside of the alternator housing. If the regulator is mounted outside (common on some Ford products) there will be a wiring harness connecting it to the alternator.

The voltage regulator controls the field current applied to the spinning rotor inside the alternator. When there is no current applied to the field, there is no voltage produced from the alternator. When voltage drops below 13.5 volts, the regulator will apply current to the field and the alternator will start charging. When the voltage exceeds 14.5 volts, the regulator will stop supplying voltage to the field and the alternator will stop charging. This is how voltage output from the alternator is regulated. When the battery is weak, the electromotive force (voltage) is not strong enough to hold back the current from the alternator trying to recharge the battery. As the battery reaches a state of full charge, the electromotive force becomes strong enough to oppose the current flow from the alternator, the amperage output from the alternator will drop to close to zero, while the voltage will remain at 13.5 to 14.5. When more electrical power is used, the electromotive force will reduce and alternator amperage will increase.

Charging System Gauge or Warning Lamp

The charging system gauge or warning lamp monitors the health of the charging system. When a charging problem is indicated，you can still drive a short distance to find help unlike an oil pressure or coolant temperature problem which can cause serious engine damage if you continue to drive.

A charging system warning lamp is a poor indicator of problems in that there are many charging problems that it will not recognize[5] . If it does light while you are driving, it usually means the charging system is not working at all. The most common cause of this is a broken alternator belt.

There are two types of gauges used to monitor charging systems on some vehicles：a voltmeter which measures system voltage or an ammeter which measures amperage. Most modern cars use a voltmeter because it is a much better indicator of charging system health.

New Words

alternator	[ˈɔːltə(ː)neitə]	n. 交流发电机
regulator	[ˈregjuleitə]	n. 调整者，校准者，调整器
charge	[tʃɑːdʒ]	n. 负荷，电荷，费用，充电
deplete	[diˈpliːt]	vt. 耗尽，使衰竭
throughout	[θru(ː)ˈaut]	prep. 遍及，贯穿；adv. 到处，始终
voltmeter	[ˈvəultˌmiːtə(r)]	n. 伏特计
ammeter	[ˈæmitə]	n. 电表
pulley	[ˈpuli]	n. 皮带轮，滑轮
serpentine	[ˈsəːpəntain]	adj. 弯曲的
periodic	[piəriˈɔdik]	adj. 周期的，定期的
magnet	[ˈmægnit]	n. 磁体，磁铁
bundle	[ˈbʌndl]	n. 捆，束，包；v. 捆扎
rotor	[ˈrəutə]	n. 转子，回转轴，转动体
stator	[ˈsteitə]	n. 定子，固定片，导轮
spin	[spin]	v. 旋转，纺，纺纱；n. 旋转
stationary	[ˈsteiʃ(ə)nəri]	adj. 固定的
evenly	[ˈiːvənli]	adv. 均匀地，平坦地
distribute	[disˈtribju(ː)t]	vt. 分发，分配，分区；v. 分发
rectifier	[ˈrektifaiə]	n. 纠正者，整顿者，校正者，整流器
diode	[ˈdaiəud]	n. 二极管
threshold	[ˈθreʃhəuld]	n. 开始，开端，极限
electromotive	[ilektrəuˈməutiv]	adj. 电测的

Phrases and Expressions

charging system	充电系统
alternating current（AC）	交流电
direct current（DC）	直流电

air conditioning compressor	空调压缩机
belt tensioner	皮带张紧器
electro magnet	电磁铁
permanent magnet	永久磁铁
make contact with	和……接触
slip ring	滑环
in other words	换句话说
rectifier assembly	整流器
voltage regulator	电压调节器
wiring harness	线束
electromotive force	电动势

Notes to the Text

音频讲解 [1]

[1]   This belt goes around a pulley connected to the front of the engine's crankshaft and is usually responsible for driving a number of other components including the water pump, power steering pump and air conditioning compressor.

这条皮带安装在发动机曲轴前端的皮带轮上，同时也用于驱动水泵、动力转向油泵和空调压缩机。

音频讲解 [2]

[2]   The rotor contains the powerful magnet that passes close to the many wire loops that make up the stator.

转子可产生一个强大的磁场，磁场穿过定子线圈。

[3]   This is done so that we can control how much voltage the alternator produces by regulating the amount of current that creates the magnetic field in the rotor.

音频讲解 [3]

这样，我们就可以通过调节转子中励磁电流的大小来控制发电机输出电压的高低。

[4]   This is accomplished by wires connected to two spring loaded brushes which rub against two slip rings on the rotor shaft.

励磁电流可以通过碳刷和滑环进入转子线圈，碳刷在弹簧的压紧力作用下与滑环摩擦接触。

音频讲解 [4]

[5]   A charging system warning lamp is a poor indicator of problems in that there are many charging problems that it will not recognize.

由于有许多故障不容易被发现，因此使用充电系统警告灯用于指示系统是否有问题。

音频讲解 [5]

Exercises

1. Answer the following questions according to the text

（1）What does the charging system consist of?

（2）What is the charging system's task?

（3）Why is the alternating current converted to direct current inside the alternator?

（4）What does it mean if warning lamp lights up while the engine is running?

（5）Are there any ideas to warn the driver if something is not right with the charging system?

（6）There are two main components that make up an alternator. What are they?

（7）How can we control the output of the alternator to suit car's needs?

（8）How we connect the current from the regulator to the spinning rotor?

2. Translate the following into Chinese

（1）refer to

（2）in the center of

（3）make contact with

（4）try to

（5）come from

（6）hold back

（7）in that

（8）at all

3. Translate the following into English

（1）充电系统

（2）皮带张紧器

（3）电磁铁

（4）永久磁铁

（5）磁场

（6）整流器

（7）电压调节器

（8）电动势

4. Fill in the blanks with the words or phrases given below, change the form where necessary

come from	than if	apply to	in other words
more than	at all	by itself	in this way

（1）On some engines, there is＿＿＿＿＿＿＿＿one belt and the task of driving these components is divided between them.

（2）More common on late model engines, one belt, called a serpentine belt will snake around the front of the engine and drive all the components＿＿＿＿＿＿＿.

（3）Take that same wire and loop it many times, ＿＿＿＿＿＿＿＿you pass the same magnet across the bundle of loops, you create a more sizable voltage in that wire.

（4）＿＿＿＿＿＿＿＿, we can control the output of the alternator to suit our needs, and protect the circuits in the automobile from excessive voltage.

（5）＿＿＿＿＿＿＿＿, we are producing alternating current in the stator.

（6）Current to generate the magnetic field in the rotor＿＿＿＿＿＿＿＿the ignition switch and passes through the voltage regulator.

（7）The voltage regulator controls the field current＿＿＿＿＿＿＿＿the spinning rotor inside the alternator.

(8) If it does light while you are driving, it usually means the charging system is not working_____.

Text B   Starting System

When the key is inserted into the ignition switch and then turned to the start position, a small amount of current then passes through the neutral safety switch to a starter relay or starter solenoid which allows high current to flow through the battery cables to the starter motor. The starter motor then cranks the engine so that the piston, moving downward, can create a suction that will draw an air-fuel mixture into the cylinder, where a spark created by the ignition system will ignite this mixture. If the compression in the engine is high enough and all this happens at the right time, the engine will start. The components of starting system are shown in Fig. 5-5.

Battery

The automotive battery is an electrochemical device that produces voltage and delivers current. In an automotive battery we can reverse the electrochemical action, thereby recharging the battery, which will then give us many years of service[1]. The purpose of the battery is to supply current to the starter motor, provide current to the ignition system while cranking, to supply additional current when the demand is higher than the alternator can supply and to act as an electrical reservoir.

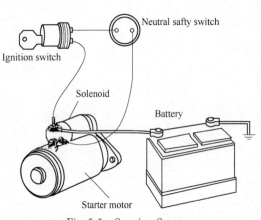

Fig. 5-5   Starting System

Ignition Switch

Most ignition switches are mounted on the steering column. The ignition switch allows the driver to distribute electrical current to where it is needed. There are generally 5 key switch positions that are used:

Lock

All circuits are open (no current supplied) and the steering wheel is in the lock position. In some cars, the transmission lever cannot be moved in this position. If the steering wheel is applying pressure to the locking mechanism, the key might be hard to turn. If you do experience this type of condition, try moving the steering wheel to remove the pressure as you turn the key[2].

Off

All circuits are open, but the steering wheel can be turned and the key cannot be extracted.

Run

All circuits, except the starter circuit, are closed (current is allowed to pass through). Current is supplied to all but the starter circuit.

Start

Power is supplied to the ignition circuit and the starter motor only. That is why the radio stops playing in the start position. This position of the ignition switch is spring loaded so that the starter is not engaged while the engine is running. This position is used momentarily, just to activate the starter.

Accessory

Power is supplied to all but the ignition and starter circuit. This allows you to play the radio, work the power windows, while the engine is not running.

Neutral Safety Switch

This switch opens (denies current to) the starter circuit when the transmission is in any gear but Neutral or Park on automatic transmissions. This switch is normally connected to the transmission linkage or directly on the transmission. Most cars utilize this same switch to apply current to the back up lights when the transmission is put in reverse. Standard transmission cars will connect this switch to the clutch pedal so that the starter will not engage unless the clutch pedal is depressed[3] . If you find that you have to move the shifter away from park or neutral to get the car to start, it usually means that this switch needs adjustment. If your car has an automatic parking brake release, the neutral safety switch will control that function also.

Starter Relay

A relay is a device that allows a small amount of electrical current to control a large amount of current. An automobile starter uses a large amount of current (250 amps) to start an engine. If we were to allow that much current to go through the ignition switch, we would not only need a very large switch, but also all the wires would have to be the size of battery cables. A starter relay is installed in series between the battery and the starter. Some cars use a starter solenoid to accomplish the same purpose of allowing a small amount of current from the ignition switch to control a high current flow from the battery to the starter. The starter solenoid in some cases also mechanically engages the starter gear with the engine.

Battery Cables

Battery cables are large diameter wire which carry the high current (250A) necessary to operate the starter motor. Some have a smaller wire soldered to the terminal which is used to either operate a smaller device or to provide an additional ground. Care must be taken to keep the battery cable ends (terminals) clean and tight. Battery cables can be replaced with ones that are slightly larger but never smaller.

Starter Motor

The starter motor is a powerful electric motor，with a small gear（pinion）attached to the end. When activated，the gear is meshed with a larger gear（ring），which is attached to the engine. The starter motor then spins the engine over so that the piston can draw in an air-fuel mixture，which is then ignited to start the engine. When the engine starts to spin faster than the starter，a device called an overrunning clutch automatically disengages the starter gear from the engine gear.

New Words

starter	['stɑːtə]	n.	起动机
relay	['riːlei]	n.	继电器
solenoid	['səulinɔid]	n.	螺线管
crank	[kræŋk]	n.	曲柄；v. 起动
reverse	[ri'vəːs]	n.	倒挡，倒退；vt. 颠倒，倒转
suction	['sʌkʃən]	n.	吸入，吸力，吸引，抽吸装置
recharge	['riː'tʃɑːdʒ]	vt.	再充电
electrical	[i'lektrik(ə)l]	adj.	电的，有关电的
reservoir	['rezəvwɑː]	n.	蓄水池，储存器
lever	['liːvə, 'levə]	n.	杆，杠杆，控制杆
momentarily	['məuməntərili]	adv.	即刻
activate	['æktiveit]	vt.	刺激，使活动；vi. 有活力
shifter	['ʃiftə]	n.	变速杆
utilize	[juː'tilaiz]	vt.	利用
pinion	['pinjən]	n.	小齿轮
mesh	[meʃ]	n.	啮合；vt. 啮合，编织

Phrases and Expressions

internal combustion engine	内燃机
connecting rod	连杆
neutral safety switch	空挡安全开关
starter relay	起动继电器
starter solenoid	起动机电磁线圈
battery cable	蓄电池电缆
back up light	倒车灯

Notes to the Text

[1] In an automotive battery we can reverse the electrochemical action，thereby recharging the battery，which will then give us many years of service.

　　汽车蓄电池的电化学过程是可逆的，因此，通过给蓄电池充电，可以持续使用多年。

音频讲解 ［1］

［2］　If you do experience this type of condition，try moving the steering wheel to remove the pressure as you turn the key.

　　如果遇到这种情况，在转动点火开关时，应该转动方向盘以消除压力。

［3］　Standard transmission cars will connect this switch to the clutch pedal so that the starter will not engage unless the clutch pedal is depressed.

音频讲解 ［2］

　　手动变速器汽车常常把这个开关安装在离合器踏板下面，这样，除非踩下踏板，否则起动机不会被起动的。

Exercises

音频讲解 ［3］

1. Translate the following abbreviations into corresponding Chinese terms

（1）ALT（alternator）

（2）B＋（battery positive）

（3）B－（battery negative）

（4）BAT（battery）

（5）CHG（charge）

（6）AC（alternating current）

（7）DC（direct current）

（8）GND（ground）

2. Translate the following sentences into Chinese

（1）The starter motor then cranks the engine so that the piston，moving downward，can create a suction that will draw an air-fuel mixture into the cylinder，where a spark created by the ignition system will ignite this mixture.

（2）The automotive battery is an electrochemical device that produces voltage and delivers current.

（3）The ignition switch allows the driver to distribute electrical current to where it is needed.

（4）If you find that you have to move the shifter away from park or neutral to get the car to start，it usually means that this switch needs adjustment.

（5）A relay is a device that allows a small amount of electrical current to control a large amount of current.

（6）Battery cables are large diameter wire which carry the high current（250A）necessary to operate the starter motor.

（7）Care must be taken to keep the battery cable ends（terminals）clean and tight.

（8）When the engine starts to spin faster than the starter，a device called an overrunning clutch automatically disengages the starter gear from the engine gear.

Workshop Manual

The Malfunctions of Charging System

There are a number of things that can go wrong with a charging system:

(1) Insufficient charging output

If one of the stator windings failed, the alternator would still charge, but only at two thirds of its normal output. Since an alternator is designed to handle all the power that is needed under heavy load conditions, you may never know that there is a problem with the unit. It might only become apparent on a dark, cold rainy night when the lights, heater, windshield wipers and possible the seat heaters and rear defroster are all on at once that you may notice the lights start to dim as you slow down. If two sets of windings failed, you will probably notice it a lot sooner.

It is more common for one or more of the six diodes in the rectifier to fail. If a diode burns out and opens one of the circuits, you would see the same problem as if one of the windings had failed. The alternator will run at a reduced output. However, if one of the diodes were to short out and allow current to pass in either direction, other problems will occur. A shorted diode will allow AC current to pass through to the automobile's electrical system, which can cause problems with the computerized sensors and processors. This condition can cause the car to act unpredictably and cause all kinds of problems.

(2) Too much voltage

A voltage regulator is designed to limit the voltage output of an alternator to 14.5 volts or less to protect the vehicle's electrical system. If the regulator malfunctions and allows uncontrolled voltage to be released, you will see bulbs and other electrical components begin to fail. This is a dangerous and potentially costly problem. Fortunately, this type of failure is very rare. Most failures cause a reduction of voltage or amperage.

(3) Noise

Since the rotor is always spinning while the engine is running, there needs to be bearings to support the shaft and allow it to spin freely. If one of those bearings were to fail, you will hear a grinding noise coming from the alternator. A mechanic's stethoscope can be used to confirm which of the spinning components driven by the serpentine belt is making the noise.

Battery Visual Inspection

(1) Make sure ignition switch is in off position and all battery feed accessories are off.

(2) Disconnect battery cables at battery (negative first).

(3) Remove battery from vehicle.

(4) Inspect the battery carrier for damage caused by the loss of acid from the battery. If acid damage is present, it will be necessary to clean the area with a solution of clean warm

water and baking soda. Scrub the area with a stiff bristle brush and wipe off with a cloth moistened with ammonia or baking soda and water.

（5）Clean the top of the battery with the same solutions as described in last step.

（6）Inspect the battery case and cover for cracks. If cracks are present, the battery must be replaced.

（7）Clean the inside surface of the terminal clamps with a suitable battery terminal cleaning tool. Replace damaged or frayed cables and broken terminal clamps.

（8）Install the battery in vehicle.

（9）Connect cable clamps to the battery post, making sure the top of the clamp is flush with top of the post.

（10）Tighten the clamp nut securely.

（11）Coat all connections with light mineral grease after tightening.

Dialogue

Introduction and Buying a Car

（C: Customer　S: Salesman）

C: I like the Honda Accord you showed me before. I think it's more practical for my needs.

S: Alright, sir. You are making a good choice. Honda has made a lot of design improvements in the new Accord.

C: What does it come with standard?

S: On all our new cars, the standard include: air conditioning, anti-lock brakes, air bags, and an AM/FM, stereo with a CD player. But on the Accord, there is another standard item as well. The Accord comes with cruise control.

C: Cruise control? I don't like that.

S: Why not, sir?

C: I think it's dangerous. What if I can't turn it off?

S: Well, sir, I know some of our customers are concerned about cruise control. But Honda has never had a single cruise control malfunction that led to an accident.

C: I wish it didn't have cruise control. My wife doesn't like it either.

S: You know, sir, you don't have to use it. You can turn it on or off. If you don't want to use it, you just never turn it on.

C: I suppose. What about the sunroof? Is that standard?

S: No, the sunroof is optional, sir.

C: I see. Another important question is the time I can get this car. I need a new car rather soon.

S: Well, I can say that the new models will be here in August. If you order one now, we will have it for you in August.

C：That's good enough，I think. What colors does the new Accord come in?

S：We have this new model in red，white，black，or silver. These are the standard colors. Of course you could specially order from various other colors too.

C：My brother has last year's Accord. And his car is a kind of soft purple color mixed with silver. I really like that color. I wonder if I can get that color on my Accord.

S：I know the color you mean. Is this it，sir?

C：Yes，I think that's it. Can I get that on the Accord?

S：Yes，you can. That color is very popular with Honda buyers. So we've kept it available.

C：Well，I think I want to order the new Accord then. It looks like an excellent car.

S：You have made a good choice，sir. I drive an Accord myself. They are very solidly built machines，very reliable.

C：Yes，I know. I think Honda is the most reliable car on the road. I would never change to anything else. The Honda I have now almost never has service problems. It runs smooth as silk.

S：Alright，sir. I will get the paperwork ready for you. Just a moment!

Automobile Transmission

Aims and Requirements

- Describe tasks of a clutch
- Explain how a clutch engages and releases
- Explain how a manual transmission works
- List the components of an automatic transmission
- List the components of torque converter
- List the components of a planetary gearset
- Translate the workshop manual
- Practice dialogues
- Cultivate students' innovative work style
- Cultivate students' teamwork spirit

Know the Structure

注释

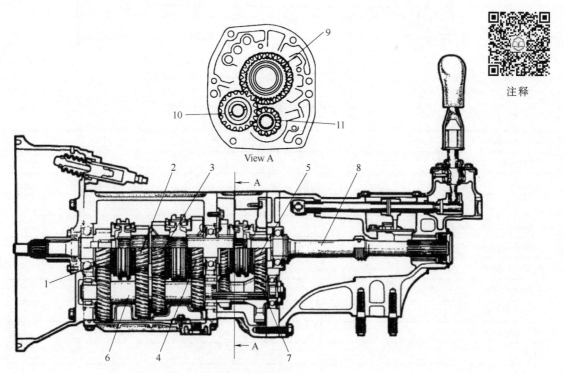

View A

Fig. 6-1   Manual Transmission

1. 4th gear	
2. 3rd gear	
3. 2nd gear	
4. 1st gear	
5. 5th gear	
6. Countershaft	
7. Counter 5th gear	
8. Mainshaft	
9. Reverse gear	
10. Reverse idle gear	
11. Counter reverse gear	

注释

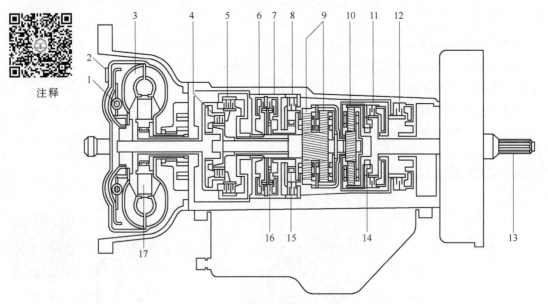

Fig. 6-2　Automatic Transmission

1. Lock-up clutch	
2. Impeller	
3. Turbine	
4. Forward drive clutch	
5. Reverse drive clutch	
6. Brake clutch	
7. Brake clutch	
8. Brake clutch	
9. Epicyclic gear set	
10. Epicyclic gear set	
11. Clutch	
12. Brake clutch	

续表

13. Output shaft	
14. Freewheel(one way clutch)	
15. Freewheel(one way clutch)	
16. Freewheel(one way clutch)	
17. Stator and one way clutch	

Text A　Clutch and Manual Transmission

Clutch

Clutch is an essential component of the transmission system that interrupts power transmission. It is installed between the engine and gearbox of an automobile. Clutches are made up of two rotating shafts. Of which one shaft is usually driven by a motor or pulley, while the other shaft is meant to drive a device[1] . A clutch links the two shafts in such a way that they can either be engaged (rotate at the same speed) or be disengaged (spin at different speeds), seeing Fig. 6-3. To engage and disengage from the flywheel in a split second is the main job of clutch. Surely, the key use of the clutch is to manage the smooth start and acceleration. Clutches are often classified as single plate friction clutch, mostly used in automobiles and trucks, or the multiple plate friction clutch, installed mostly in diesel engines and motorcycles. Further, they can also be classified as "wet" or "dry" depending on whether they are immersed in a lubricating fluid or not[2] .

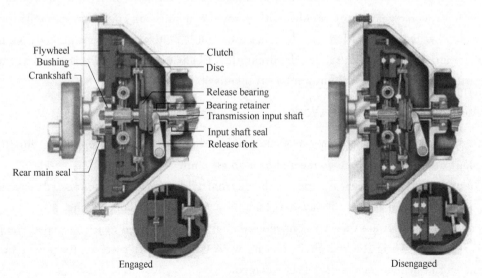

Fig. 6-3　Clutch of Geely Car

How a Clutch Engages and Releases

In an automobile clutch, the flywheel is connected to the engine, and the clutch plate is connected to the transmission. When your foot is off the pedal，the springs push the pressure plate against the clutch disc，which in turn presses against the flywheel. This locks the engine to the transmission input shaft，making them spin at the same speed.

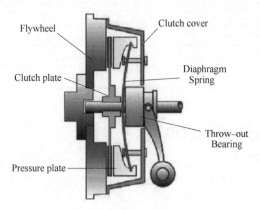

Fig. 6-4 Clutch Pedal is Pressed

When the clutch pedal is pressed，a cable or hydraulic piston pushes on the release fork，which presses the throw-out bearing against the middle of the diaphragm spring. As the middle of the diaphragm spring is pushed in，a series of pins near the outside of the spring causes the spring to pull the pressure plate away from the clutch disc. This releases the clutch from the spinning engine，seeing Fig. 6-4.

Transmission

Automobile transmission can either be manual or automatic. The manual transmissions feature different gear ratios which can be switched to by engaging pairs of gears inside the transmission. A driver drives the vehicle with the help of a hand-operated gearshift and a foot operated clutch. A manual transmission system is known by several different terms such as standard transmission，stick shift，stick，or straight drive[3] . On the other hand the automatic transmissions typically have gears controlled by brake bands or clutch packs for selecting a gear ratio.

Although，the current automobile transmissions comprise a set of four to six forward gears with a reverse gear，automobiles with manual transmission consisting of eight forward gears have also been built. Manual，Automatic，Non-synchronous，Continuously variable，Semi-automatic，Infinitely variable，Hydrostatic，Electric variable，Electric and Hydrodynamic are some other types of automobile transmission systems.

How Manual Transmissions Work

As shown in Fig. 6-5，the green shaft comes from the engine through the clutch. The green shaft and green gear are connected as a single unit.

The red shaft and gears are called the layshaft. These are also connected as a single piece，so all of the gears on the layshaft and the layshaft itself spin as one unit. The green shaft and the red shaft are directly connected through their meshed gears so that if the green shaft is spinning，so is the red shaft. In this way，the layshaft receives its power directly from the engine whenever the clutch is engaged.

The yellow shaft is a spline shaft that connects directly to the drive shaft through the differential to the drive wheels of the car. If the wheels are spinning，the yellow shaft is spinning.

The blue gears ride on bearings，so they spin on the yellow shaft. If the engine is off but

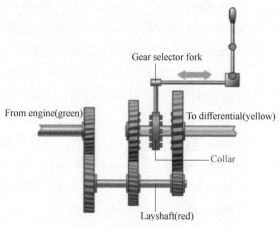

Fig. 6-5   How Manual Transmission Work

the car is coasting，the yellow shaft can turn inside the blue gears while the blue gears and the layshaft are motionless.

The purpose of the collar is to connect one of the two blue gears to the yellow drive shaft. The collar is connected，through the splines，directly to the yellow shaft and spins with the yellow shaft. However，the collar can slide left or right along the yellow shaft to engage either of the blue gears. Teeth on the collar fit into holes on the sides of the blue gears to engage them[4] .

When the collar is between the two gears，the transmission is in neutral. Both of the blue gears freewheel on the yellow shaft at the different rates controlled by their ratios to the layshaft[5] .

New Words

clutch	[klʌtʃ]	n. 离合器
essential	[i'senʃəl]	adj. 本质的，主要的，最重要的
transmission	[trænz'miʃən]	n. 传动，传送
interrupt	[intə'rʌpt]	vt. 阻断，阻止，打扰
install	[in'stɔːl]	v. 安装，装配
gearbox	[giəbɔks]	n. 齿轮箱，变速箱
disengage	[disin'geidʒ]	v. 分离，断开，切断
surely	[ʃuəli]	adj. 的确，当然
mileage	[mailidʒ]	n. 汽车消耗 1 加仑汽油所行驶的平均里程 [1 加仑（英）为 4.546dm^3]
classify	['klæsifai]	vt. 分类，分级
immerse	[i'məːs]	v. 浸入，浸渍，泡
cable	['keibl]	n. 绳，缆，钢索
hydraulic	[hai'drɔːlik]	adj. 液压的
gearshift	[giəʃift]	n. 换挡，变速器

comprise	[kəm'praiz]	*vt*. 包括，由……组成
non-synchronous	[nɔn'siŋkrənəs]	*adj*. 非同步的，异步的，不同期的
variable	['vɛəriəbl]	*n*. 变量，变数
hydrostatic	[haidrɔ'stætik]	*adj*. 液压静力的，流体静力的
layshaft	['leiʃɑːft]	*n*. 副轴，侧轴，中间轴
differential	[difə'reʃəl]	*n*. 差速器
coasting	['kəustiŋ]	*n*. 滑行，惯性运动
motionless	['məuʃənis]	*adj*. 不动的，静止的，固定的
collar	['kɔlə]	*n*. 法兰盘，联轴节，轴衬，环
neutral	['njuːtrəl]	*n*. 空挡

Phrases and Expressions

manual transmission	手动变速器
a split second	一瞬间，一刹那
single plate friction clutch	单片式摩擦离合器
multiple plate friction clutch	多片式摩擦离合器
release fork	释放叉，分离叉
throw-out bearing	分离轴承，推力轴承
diaphragm spring	膜片弹簧
pressure plate	压盘
clutch disc	离合器从动盘
gear ratio	齿数比，齿轮传动比
switch to	转到，换到
brake band	制动带
forward gear	前进挡
reverse gear	倒挡
spline shaft	花键轴
drive shaft	传动轴

Notes to the Text

音频讲解 [1]

[1]　Of which one shaft is usually driven by a motor or pulley，while the other shaft is meant to drive a device.

　　两轴中的一个轴，通常是由发动机或带轮驱动的，而另一根轴用于驱动其它设备。

音频讲解 [2]

[2]　Further，they can also be classified as "wet" or "dry" depending on whether they are immersed in a lubricating fluid or not.

　　而且，离合器依据是否浸在油中而分为湿式和干式两种。

［3］ A manual transmission system is known by several different terms such as standard transmission，stick shift，stick，or straight drive.

手动变速箱有几种不同的名称，如：标准传动、手动换挡、手动挡、直接传动等。

音频讲解 ［3］

［4］ Teeth on the collar fit into holes on the sides of the blue gears to engage them.

套筒上的齿刚好卡进蓝色齿轮上的孔，以便和蓝色齿轮啮合。

音频讲解 ［4］

［5］ Both of the blue gears freewheel on the yellow shaft at the different rates controlled by their ratios to the layshaft.

两个蓝色齿轮都在黄色轴上自由转动，速率是由中间轴上的齿轮和蓝色齿轮间的变速比决定的。

音频讲解 ［5］

Exercises

1. Answer the following questions according to the text

（1） Why do we need the clutch?

（2） Do you know the main job of the clutch?

（3） How do you classify clutches?

（4） How does the clutch work?

（5） How does the clutch engage and release?

（6） How does manual transmission work?

（7） What is the purpose of the collar?

（8） When is the transmission in neutral?

2. Translate the following into Chinese

（1） a split second

（2） clutch cover

（3） neutral gear

（4） clutch thrust bearing

（5） friction clutch

（6） semi-automatic transmission

（7） spline shaft

（8） switch to

3. Translate the following into English

（1） 膜片弹簧离合器

（2） 单片式离合器

（3） 挂挡

（4） 压盘

（5） 离合器壳

（6） 前进挡

（7） 倒挡

（8） 一挡

4. Fill in the blanks with the words or phrases given below，change the form where necessary

come from	a series of	such as	on the other hand
depend on	in this way	in turn	fit into

（1）They can also be classified as "wet" or "dry" _____ whether they are immersed in a lubricating fluid or not.

（2）When your foot is off the pedal，the springs push the pressure plate against the clutch disc，which_____presses against the flywheel.

（3）As the middle of the diaphragm spring is pushed in，_____pins near the outside of the spring causes the spring to pull the pressure plate away from the clutch disc.

（4）A manual transmission is known by different terms_____standard transmission，stick shift，stick，or straight drive.

（5）_____the automatic transmissions typically have gears controlled by brake bands or clutch packs for selecting a gear ratio.

（6）The green shaft_____the engine through the clutch.

（7）_____，the layshaft receives its power directly from the engine whenever the clutch is engaged.

（8）Teeth on the collar_____holes on the sides of the blue gears to engage them.

Text B　Automatic Transmission

An automatic transmission performs the same functions as a standard transmission. However，it "shifts gears" and "releases the clutch" automatically. A majority of modern cars use an automatic transmission（or transaxle）because it saves the driver from having to move a shift lever and depress a clutch pedal[1] .

An automatic transmission normally senses engine speeds（rpm）and engine load（engine vacuum or throttle position）to determine gear shift points. It then uses internal oil pressure to shift gears. Computers can also be used to sense or control automatic transmission shift points.

Refer to Fig. 6-6 as the following parts of an automatic transmission are introduced.

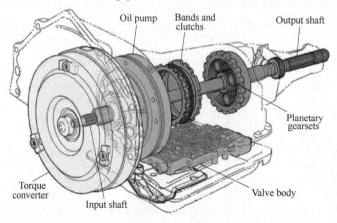

Fig. 6-6　Automatic Transmission

（1）Torque converter—fluid coupling that connects and disconnects engine and transmission.

（2）Input shaft—transfers power from torque converter to internal drive members and gearsets.

（3）Oil pump—produces pressure to operate hydraulic components in transmission.

（4）Valve body—operated by shift lever and sensors, controls oil flow to pistons and servos.

（5）Pistons and servos—actuate bands and clutches.

（6）Bands and clutches—apply clamping or driving pressure on different parts of gearsets to operate them.

（7）Planetary gearsets—provide different gear ratios and reverse gear.

（8）Output shaft—transfers engine torque from gearsets to drive shaft, and rear wheels.

An automatic transmission uses three methods to transmit power: fluid, friction, and gears. The torque converter uses fluid to transfer power. The bands and clutches use friction. The transmission gears, not only transmit power, they can increase or decrease speed and torque[2] .

Torque Converter

The torque converter is a fluid clutch that performs the same basic function as a manual transmission's dry friction clutch. It provides a means of uncoupling the engine for stopping the car in gear. It also provides a means of coupling the engine for acceleration.

Two house fans can be used to demonstrate the basic action inside a torque converter. Look at Fig. 6-7. One fan is plugged in and is spinning. The other fan is not plugged into electrical power.

Since the whirling fan is facing the other, it can be used to spin the unplugged fan, transferring power through a liquid (air) . This same principle applies inside a torque converter, but oil is used instead of air.

A torque converter consists of four basic parts: the outer housing, an impeller or pump, a turbine, and a stator. These parts are shown in Fig. 6-8.

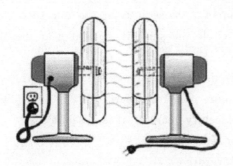

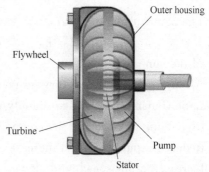

Fig. 6-7　Two Fans Demonstrate Principle of
Fluid Coupling or Torque Converter

Fig. 6-8　Torque Converter

The impeller, stator, and turbine have curved or curled fan blades. They work like our simple example of one fan driving another. The impeller drives the turbine.

Automatic Transmission Shaft

Typically, an automatic transmission has two main shafts: the input shaft and output shaft.

An automatic transmission input shaft or turbine shaft connects the torque converter with the driving components in the transmission.

Each end of the input shaft has external splines. These splines fit into splines in the torque converter turbine and a driving unit in the transmission[3]. The input shaft rides on bushings. Transmission fluid lubricates the shaft and bushings.

The output shaft connects the driving components in the transmission with the drive shaft. This shaft runs in the same centerline as the input shaft. Its front end almost touches the input shaft.

Planetary Gears

A planetary gearset consists of a sun gear, several planet gears, a planet gear carrier, and a ring gear. A simple planetary gearset is shown in Fig. 6-9.

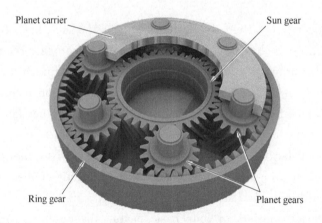

Fig. 6-9 Planetary Gearset

The name planetary gearset is easy to remember because it refers to our solar system. Just as our planets (Earth, Jupiter, Mars) circle the sun, the planet gears revolve around the sun gear[4].

As you can see, a planetary gearset is always in mesh. It is very strong and compact. An automatic transmission will commonly use two or more planetary gearsets.

By holding or releasing the components of a planetary gearset, it is possible to:

Reduce output speed and increase torque (gear reduction).

Increase output speed while lowering torque (overdrive).

Reverse output direction (reverse gear).

Serve as a solid unit to transfer power（one to one ratio）.

Freewheel to stop power flow（park or neutral）.

Hydraulic System

The hydraulic system for an automatic transmission typically consists of a pump，pressure regulator，manual valve，vacuum modulator valve，governor valve，shift valves，servos，pistons，and valve body. These parts work together to form the "brain"（sensing）and "muscles"（control）of an automatic transmission.

The hydraulic system also forces oil to high friction points in the transmission. This prevents wear and overheating by lubricating the moving parts.

New Words

majority	[mə'dʒɔriti]	n. 多数，大半
servo	['səːvəu]	n. 伺服，伺服系统
clamp	[klæmp]	vt. 夹住，夹紧
actuate	['æktjueit]	vt. 开动，促使
demonstrate	['demənstreit]	vt. 示范，证明，论证
whirl	[(h)wəːl]	v.（使）旋转，急动，急走
impeller	[im'pelə]	n. 推进者，叶轮，泵轮
turbine	['təːbin, - bain]	n. 涡轮
curve	[kəːv]	vt. 弯，使弯曲
curl	[kəːl]	v.（使）卷曲
blade	[bleid]	n. 刀片，叶片
bushing	['buʃiŋ]	n. 轴衬，衬套
centerline	['sentəlain]	n. 中心线
Jupiter	['dʒuːpitə]	n. 木星
Mars	[maːz]	n. 火星
overdrive	['əuvə'draiv]	vt. 超速传动

Phrases and Expressions

shift lever	换挡杆
oil pressure	油压，机油压力
torque converter	液力变矩器
planetary gearset	行星齿轮组
sun gear	太阳轮
planet gear	行星轮
planet gear carrier	行星架
ring gear	齿圈，齿环
fluid coupling	液力偶合器
valve body	阀体

dry friction clutch	干式摩擦离合器
fan blade	风扇叶片
external spline	外花键
pressure regulator	压力调节器
manual valve	手控阀
vacuum modulator valve	真空调节阀
governor valve	调速阀
shift valve	换挡阀

Notes to the Text

音频讲解 [1]

[1] A majority of modern cars use an automatic transmission（or transaxle）because it saves the driver from having to move a shift lever and depress a clutch pedal.

现代的大多数汽车使用自动变速器（或变速驱动桥），因为这样驾驶员就可以不用操纵变速杆和离合器踏板。

音频讲解 [2]

[2] The transmission gears, not only transmit power, they can increase or decrease speed and torque.

变速器齿轮不仅能够传递能量，也能增大或降低转速和扭矩。

音频讲解 [3]

[3] These splines fit into splines in the torque converter turbine and a driving unit in the transmission.

输入轴两端的外花键分别与变矩器涡轮和变速器驱动部件的内花键相啮合。

音频讲解 [4]

[4] Just as our planets（Earth, Jupiter, Mars）circle the sun, the planet gears revolve around the sun gear.

就像行星（地球，木星，火星）围绕太阳转一样，行星齿轮围绕着太阳轮旋转。

Exercises

1. Translate the following abbreviations into corresponding Chinese terms

（1）CL（clutch）

（2）HTC（hydraulic torque converter）

（3）MT（manual transmission）

（4）AT（automatic transmission）

（5）CVT（continuously variable transmission）

（6）DCT（dual clutch transmission）

（7）AMT（automatic manual transmission）

（8）ATF（automatic transmission fluid）

2. Translate the following sentences into Chinese

（1）An automatic transmission performs the same functions as a standard transmission.

（2）An automatic transmission normally senses engine speeds（rpm）and engine load (engine vacuum or throttle position) to determine gear shift points.

(3) The torque converter is a fluid clutch that performs the same basic function as a manual transmission's dry friction clutch.

(4) Since the whirling fan is facing the other, it can be used to spin the unplugged fan, transferring power through a liquid (air) .

(5) A torque converter consists of four basic parts: the outer housing, an impeller or pump, a turbine, and a stator.

(6) A planetary gearset consists of a sun gear, several planet gears, a planet gear carrier, and a ring gear.

(7) The name planetary gearset is easy to remember because it refers to our solar system.

(8) The hydraulic system for an automatic transmission typically consists of a pump, pressure regulator, manual valve, vacuum modulator valve, governor valve, shift valves, servos, pistons, and valve body.

Workshop Manual

Manual Transmission Removal and Installation

(1) Remove the battery, battery tray and battery bracket.

(2) Remove the air cleaner component.

(3) Remove the wheels, tires and splash shields.

(4) Remove the auto under cover.

(5) Remove the steering gear and power steering pipe.

(6) Remove the front auto leveling sensor.

(7) Drain the transmission oil into a suitable container.

(8) Remove in the order indicated in the table.

(9) Install in the reverse order of removal.

(10) Adjust the headlight zero set.

(11) Add the specified amount of specified transmission oil.

(12) Install the air cleaner component.

(13) Warm up the engine and transmission, inspect for oil leakage, and inspect the transmission operation.

ZF4HP22 Transmission

The ZF4HP22 transmission is used on 2. 5 liter Diesel and 4. 0 liter petrol models. 4. 6 liter petrol models use the ZF4HP24 transmission unit to accomodate the increased power output of the larger engine. Both units are of similar construction with the ZF4HP24 unit being slightly longer. The operation of both units is the same.

Automatic transmission vehicles are fitted with an H-gate selector mechanism. The selector mechanism combines the operation of the transmission selector lever and the transfer box high/low gear range selection. Selections on the selector lever assembly are transmitted by a selector cable to a gear position switch.

The gear position switch on the transmission passes gear selection signals to an electronic automatic transmission (EAT) ECU located below the left front seat, which outputs the appropriate control signals to an electro-hydraulic valve block in the transmission. A mode switch enables the driver to change the control mode of the EAT ECU between manual, economy and sport. The EAT ECU provides signals to the message center in the instrument pack to indicate the control mode and system status.

The gearbox features a pressure lubrication system and is cooled by pumping the lubricant through an oil cooler located in front of the engine cooling radiator.

Petrol models feature a revised EAT ECU with controller area network (CAN) digital communications between the EAT ECU and the ECM.

Dialogue

Purchasing Autos Online

(C: Customer S: Salesman)

C: Hey, Sir. I came across a new word e-commerce, when I browsed the internet this morning. Have you heard of it?

S: Yes. E-commerce means electronic commerce. On the internet, people like to use just one letter to represent something. For example, you can talk about "e-commerce" and talk about "B to B e-commerce" or "B to C e-commerce" . "B to B" means "business to business", businesses selling things to businesses. "B to C" would be "business to consumer" .

C: That's interesting. So tell me more about e-commerce.

S: E-commerce is very popular now all over the world. And that means buying and selling things for businesses and consumers on the internet.

C: Really? Buying and selling things online?

S: That's right. Today, we can even buy autos online.

C: That's great. I just want to buy a new car. Can you tell me more about it? Maybe I will purchase a car online.

S: Sure. You can buy a car at an auto dealer's web site, but for some technical and financial reasons, you can't complete all steps online. The data from the sites can help you decide on make, model and price. Most sites let customers complete credit applications, schedule sales and service appointments and visit automaker web pages.

Automobile Steering System

Aims and Requirements

- List the components of steering system
- List the most common types of steering gear
- Describe the tasks of rack-and-pinion gearset
- Explain how a recirculating-ball steering works
- List the key components of power steering system
- Translate the workshop manual
- Practice dialogues
- Cultivate students' good professional ethics
- Cultivate students' learning habits of independent thinking

Know the Structure

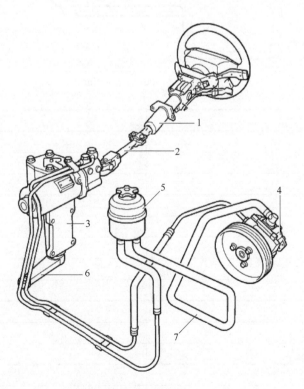

注释

Fig. 7-1　Steering System

1. Steering column	
2. Steering column intermediate shaft	
3. Steering box	
4. Hydraulic pump	
5. Oil reservoir	
6. Drop arm	
7. Hydraulic pipes	

注释

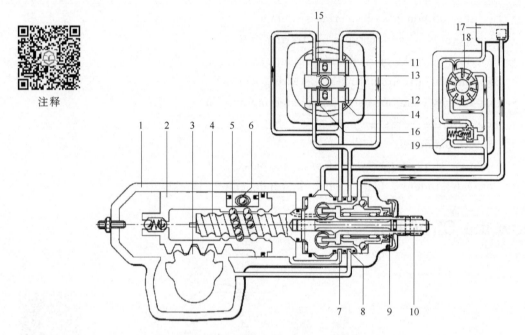

Fig. 7-2   Power Steering System

1. Steering housing	
2. Piston	
3. Sector shaft	
4. Worm	
5. Recirculating balls	
6. Recirculating tube	
7. Radial groove	
8. Radial groove	
9. Input shaft	
10. Torsion bar	
11. Valve spool	
12. Valve spool	
13. Inlet grooves	
14. Inlet grooves	

15. Return grooves	
16. Return grooves	
17. Fluid reservoir	
18. Hydraulic pump	
19. Pressure and flow limiting valve	

Text A   Steering System

The purpose of steering system is guiding the car where the driver wants it to go[1]. The manual steering system consists of steering wheel, steering column, a manual gearbox, pitman arm, drag link, steering knuckle arm, king pin, steering arms, tie rod, front axle and steering knuckle. They enable the car to change the direction by means of turning and moving forth and back.

Turning the Car

When you turn your car, your front wheels are not pointing in the same direction (See Fig. 7-3).

For a car to turn smoothly, each wheel must follow a different circle. Since the inside wheel is following a circle with a smaller radius, it is actually making a tighter turn than the outside wheel[2]. If you draw a line perpendicular to each wheel, the lines will intersect at the center point of the turn. The geometry of the steering linkage makes the inside wheel turn more than the outside wheel.

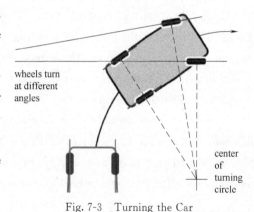

Fig. 7-3   Turning the Car

Steering Gear

The steering gear is a device for converting the rotary motion of the steering wheel into straight-line motion of linkage. There are several manual steering systems gears in current use, the most common are "rack and pinion" type and "recirculating ball" type.

Rack-and-pinion Steering

Rack-and-pinion steering is quickly becoming the most common type of steering on cars, small trucks and SUVs. It is actually a pretty simple mechanism. A rack-and-pinion gearset is enclosed in a metal tube, with each end of the rack protruding from the tube. A rod, called a tie rod, connects to each end of the rack.

The pinion gear is attached to the steering shaft. When you turn the steering wheel, the

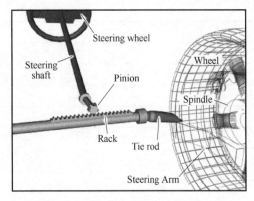

Fig. 7-4　Rack-and-pinion Steering

gear spins, moving the rack. The tie rod at each end of the rack connects to the steering arm on the spindle (see Fig. 7-4).

The rack-and-pinion gearset does two things:

(1) It converts the rotational motion of the steering wheel into the linear motion needed to turn the wheels[3].

(2) It provides a gear reduction, making it easier to turn the wheels.

On most cars, it takes three to four complete revolutions of the steering wheel to make the wheels turn from lock to lock (from far left to far right).

The steering ratio is the ratio of how far you turn the steering wheel to how far the wheels turn. For instance, if one complete revolution (360 degrees) of the steering wheel results in the wheels of the car turning 20 degrees, then the steering ratio is 360 divided by 20, or 18 : 1[4].

A higher ratio means that you have to turn the steering wheel more to get the wheels to turn a given distance. However, less effort is required because of the higher gear ratio.

Generally, lighter, sports cars have lower steering ratios than larger cars and trucks. The lower ratio gives the steering a quicker response (you don't have to turn the steering wheel as much to get the wheels to turn a given distance), which is a desirable trait in sports cars. These smaller cars are light enough that even with the lower ratio, the effort required to turn the steering wheel is not excessive.

Some cars have variable-ratio steering, which uses a rack-and-pinion gearset that has a different tooth pitch (number of teeth per inch) in the center than it has on the outside[5]. This makes the car respond quickly when starting a turn (the rack is near the center), and also reduces effort near the wheel's turning limits.

Recirculating-ball Steering

Recirculating-ball steering (see Fig. 7-5) is used on many trucks and SUVs today. The linkage that turns the wheels is slightly different than on a rack-and-pinion system.

The recirculating-ball steering gear contains a worm gear. You can image the gear in two parts. The first part is a block of metal with a threaded hole in it. This block has gear teeth cut into the outside of it, which engage a gear that moves the pitman arm. The steering wheel connects to a threaded rod, similar to a bolt, which sticks into the hole in the block. When the steering wheel turns, it turns the bolt. Instead of twisting further into the block the way a regular bolt would, this bolt is held fixed so that when it spins, it moves the block, which moves the gear that turns the wheels[6].

Instead of the bolt directly engaging the threads in the block, all of the threads are filled

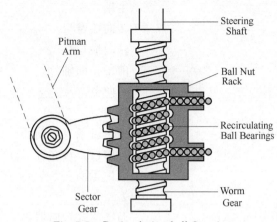

Fig. 7-5 Recirculating-ball Steering

with ball bearings that recirculate through the gear as it turns. The balls actually serve two purposes. First，they reduce friction and wear in the gear. Second，they reduce slap in the gear.

New Words

radius	['reidjəs]	n. 半径
perpendicular	[ˌpəːpən'dikjulə]	adj. 垂直的，正交的；n. 垂线
intersect	[ˌintə'sekt]	vi. (直线) 相交，交叉
geometry	[dʒi'ɔmitri]	n. 几何学
rack	[ræk]	n. 架，齿条
recirculate	[ri'səːkjuleit]	v. 再通行，再流通
protrude	[prə'truːd]	v. 突出
gearset	['giəset]	n. 齿轮组，变速箱
desirable	[di'zaiərəbl]	adj. 值得要的，合意的
trait	[treit]	n. 显著的特点，特性
pitch	[pitʃ]	n. 程度
spindle	['spindl]	n. 轴，心轴
rotational	[rəu'teiʃənəl]	adj. 转动的，循环的
stick	[stik]	v. 粘住，粘贴；vt. 刺，戳
engage	[in'geidʒ]	vi. 接合，啮合
thread	[θred]	n. 螺纹
slap	[slæp]	n. 拍，掌击，拍击声

Phrases and Expressions

steering wheel	方向盘
steering column	转向柱，转向杆
pitman arm	转向摇臂
drag link	转向直拉杆

king pin	主销
steering arm	转向摇臂
tie rod	转向横拉杆
front axle	前桥，前轴
steering knuckle	转向节
steering gear	转向器
rack and pinion steering gear	齿轮齿条式转向器
steering shaft	转向柱，转向杆
linear motion	线性运动
tooth pitch	齿距
recirculating ball steering gear	循环球式转向器
SUV（sport utility vehicle）	运动型多用途车
worm gear	蜗轮
threaded hole	螺纹孔
threaded rod	螺杆

Notes to the Text

音频讲解 [1]

[1]　The purpose of steering system is guiding the car where the driver wants it to go.

转向系统的用途是在驾驶员的操纵下控制汽车行驶的方向。

[2]　Since the inside wheel is following a circle with a smaller radius, it is actually making a tighter turn than the outside wheel.

由于内侧车轮转弯半径更小，因此内侧车轮要比外侧车轮偏转角度更大。

音频讲解 [2]

[3]　It converts the rotational motion of the steering wheel into the linear motion needed to turn the wheels.

它把方向盘的旋转运动转变成车轮转向所需的直线运动。

音频讲解 [3]

[4]　For instance, if one complete revolution（360 degrees）of the steering wheel results in the wheels of the car turning 20 degrees, then the steering ratio is 360 divided by 20, or 18：1.

例如，方向盘转一周（360°），使车轮转 20°的话，那么其角传动比就是 360 除以 20，或 18：1。

音频讲解 [4]

[5]　Some cars have variable-ratio steering, which uses a rack-and-pinion gearset that has a different tooth pitch（number of teeth per inch）in the center than it has on the outside.

有些车的角传动比是可变的，它采用齿轮齿条式转向器，齿条中间与外侧的齿距（每英寸的齿数）是不同的。

[6]　Instead of twisting further into the block the way a regular bolt would, this bolt is held fixed so that when it spins, it moves the block, which moves the gear that turns the wheels.

音频讲解 [6]

　　与通常的螺栓旋入螺母不同，循环球式转向器的螺杆是固定的，当它旋转时，螺母沿着螺杆移动，从而带动车轮偏转。

Exercises

1. Answer the following questions according to the text

（1）What are the functions of a steering system?

（2）What is the most common steering?

（3）What are the components of a steering system?

（4）How does the Rack-and-pinion gearset work?

（5）How many tasks does the Rack-and-pinion gearset do? What are they?

（6）What is the steering ratio?

（7）How does the recirculating-ball steering gearset work?

（8）What is the function of the steering linkages?

2. Translate the following into Chinese

（1）pitman arm

（2）drag link

（3）tie rod

（4）rack and pinion steering gear

（5）recirculating ball steering gear

（6）steering shaft

（7）steering knuckle

（8）steering radius

3. Translate the following into English

（1）线性运动

（2）旋转运动

（3）方向盘

（4）转向节臂

（5）转向机构

（6）扇形齿轮

（7）转向摇臂

（8）转向器

4. Fill in the blanks with the words or phrases given below, change the form where necessary

result in	instead of	connect to	by means of
more than	because of	attach to	steering ratio

（1）They enable the car to change the direction＿＿＿＿＿turning and moving forth and back.

（2）The steering linkage makes the inside wheel turn＿＿＿＿＿the outside wheel.

（3）A rod，called a tie rod，＿＿＿＿＿each end of the rack.

（4）The pinion gear is＿＿＿＿＿the steering shaft.

（5）The＿＿＿＿＿is the ratio of how far you turn the steering wheel to how far the wheels turn.

(6) If one complete revolution of the steering wheel_____the wheels of the car turning 20 degrees, then the steering ratio is 360 divided by 20, or 18 : 1.

(7) However, less effort is required_____the higher gear ratio.

(8) _____the bolt directly engaging the threads in the block, all of the threads are filled with ball bearings that recirculate through the gear as it turns.

Text B   Power Steering

Power steering systems normally use an engine-driven pump and hydraulic system to assist steering action. Pressure from the oil pump is used to operate a piston and cylinder assembly. When the control valve routes oil pressure into one end of the piston, the piston

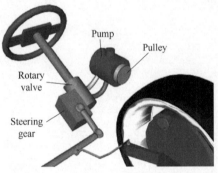

slides in its cylinder. Piston movement can then be used to help move the steering system components and front wheels of the vehicles.

There are a couple of key components in power steering in addition to the rack-and-pinion or recirculating-ball mechanism, Seeing Fig. 7-6.

Fig. 7-6   A Power Steering System

Pump

The hydraulic power for the steering is provided by a rotary vane pump, seeing Fig. 7-7. This pump is driven by the car's engine via a belt and pulley. It contains a set of retractable vanes that spin inside an oval chamber.

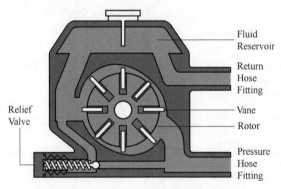

Fig. 7-7   A Rotary Vane Pump

As the vanes spin, they pull hydraulic fluid from the return line at low pressure and force it into the outlet at high pressure[1] . The amount of flow provided by the pump depends on the car's engine speed. The pump must be designed to provide adequate flow when the engine is idling. As a result, the pump moves much more fluid than necessary when the engine is running at faster speeds.

The pump contains a pressure-relief valve to make sure that the pressure does not get too high, especially at high engine speeds when so much fluid is being pumped.

Rotary Valve

A power-steering system should assist the driver only when he is exerting force on the steering wheel (such as when starting a turn). When the driver is not exerting force (such as when driving in a straight line), the system shouldn't provide any assist. The device that senses the force on the steering wheel is called the rotary valve, seeing Fig. 7-8.

The key to the rotary valve is a torsion bar. The torsion bar is a thin rod of metal that twists when torque is applied to it[2]. The top of the bar is connected to the steering wheel, and the bottom of the bar is connected to the pinion or worm gear (which turns the wheels), so the amount of torque in the torsion bar is equal to the amount of torque the driver is using to turn the wheels. The more torque the driver uses to turn the wheels, the more the bar twists.

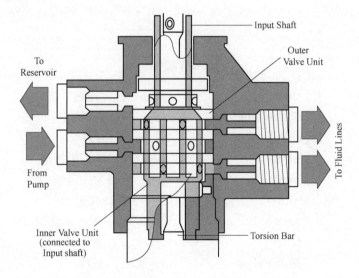

Fig. 7-8   Rotary Valve

The input from the steering shaft forms the inner part of a spool valve assembly. It also connects to the top end of the torsion bar. The bottom of the torsion bar connects to the outer part of the spool valve. The torsion bar also turns the output of the steering gear, connecting to either the pinion gear or the worm gear depending on which type of steering the car has[3].

As the bar twists, it rotates the inside of the spool valve relative to the outside. Since the inner part of the spool valve is also connected to the steering shaft (and therefore to the steering wheel), the amount of rotation between the inner and outer parts of the spool valve depends on how much torque the driver applies to the steering wheel.

When the steering wheel is not being turned, both hydraulic lines provide the same amount of pressure to the steering gear. But if the spool valve is turned one way or the other, ports open up to provide high-pressure fluid to the appropriate line.

The Future of Power Steering

Since the power-steering pump on most cars today runs constantly，pumping fluid all the time，it wastes horsepower. This wasted power translates into wasted fuel.

You can expect to see several innovations that will improve fuel economy. One of the coolest ideas on the drawing board is the "steer-by-wire" or "drive-by-wire" system[4]. These systems would completely eliminate the mechanical connection between the steering wheel and the steering，replacing it with a purely electronic control system. It would contain sensors that tell the car what the driver is doing with the wheel，and have some motors in it to provide the driver with feedback on what the car is doing[5]. The output of these sensors would be used to control a motorized steering system. This would free up space in the engine compartment by eliminating the steering shaft. It would also reduce vibration inside the car.

In the past fifty years，car steering systems haven't changed much. But in the next decade，we'll see advances in car steering that will result in more efficient cars and a more comfortable ride.

New Words

via	[ˈvaiə, ˈviːə]	prep.	经，通过，经由
retractable	[riˈtræktəbl]	adj.	可收回的
vane	[vein]	n.	翼，叶片
oval	[ˈəuvəl]	adj.	卵形的，椭圆的
adequate	[ˈædikwit]	adj.	适当的，足够的
idle	[ˈaidl]	vi.	空转，急速
sense	[sens]	vt.	感到，理解，认识
twist	[twist]	vt.	拧，扭曲；vi. 扭弯，扭曲
innovation	[ˌinəuˈveiʃən]	n.	改革，创新
feedback	[ˈfiːdbæk]	n.	反馈，反应

Phrases and Expressions

power steering	动力转向
rotary vane pump	旋转叶片泵
pressure-relief valve	卸压阀
rotary valve	旋转阀
torsion bar	扭力杆
spool valve	伺服阀
relative to	相对，相关
on the drawing board	在设计阶段，在筹划之中

Notes to the Text

[1] As the vanes spin，they pull hydraulic fluid from the return line at

音频讲解 [1]

low pressure and force it into the outlet at high pressure.

随着叶片旋转，叶片泵将液压油从低压回油管吸入，增压后从高压出口排出。

〔2〕　The torsion bar is a thin rod of metal that twists when torque is applied to it.

扭力杆是一种细金属杆，施加扭矩时就会发生扭曲。

〔3〕　The torsion bar also turns the output of the steering gear，connecting to either the pinion gear or the worm gear depending on which type of steering the car has.

扭力杆驱动转向器的输出部件，根据汽车转向器型式不同，该部件与小齿轮或涡轮相连。

〔4〕　One of the coolest ideas on the drawing board is the "steer-by-wire" or "drive-by-wire" system.

设计中最酷的想法就是"线控转向"或者"线控驱动"系统。

〔5〕　It would contain sensors that tell the car what the driver is doing with the wheel，and have some motors in it to provide the driver with feedback on what the car is doing.

线控系统具有能够反应驾驶员操控方向盘意图的传感器，以及能够给驾驶员提供车辆反馈信息的驱动电机。

Exercises

1. Translate the following abbreviations into corresponding Chinese terms

（1）STRG（steering）

（2）PS（power steering）

（3）PSP（power steering pressure）

（4）PSC（power steering control）

（5）4WS（four wheel steering）

（6）SAS（steering angle sensor）

（7）SCCM（steering column control module）

（8）ESP（electronic stability program）

2. Translate the following sentences into Chinese

（1）Power steering systems normally use an engine-driven pump and hydraulic system to assist steering action.

（2）There are a couple of key components in power steering in addition to the rack-and-pinion or recirculating-ball mechanism.

（3）It contains a set of retractable vanes that spin inside an oval chamber.

（4）As a result，the pump moves much more fluid than necessary when the engine is running at faster speeds.

（5）The pump contains a pressure-relief valve to make sure that the pressure does not get too high，especially at high engine speeds when so much fluid is being pumped.

（6）The top of the bar is connected to the steering wheel，and the bottom of the bar is connected to the pinion or worm gear，so the amount of torque in the torsion bar is equal to the amount of torque the driver is using to turn the wheels.

（7）Since the power-steering pump on most cars today runs constantly，pumping fluid all the time，it wastes horsepower.

（8）But in the next decade，we'll see advances in car steering that will result in more efficient cars and a more comfortable ride.

Workshop Manual

Heavy Steering

Possible Cause	Remedy
1. Insufficient power assistance.	1. Carry out PAS Test to check cause and rectify as necessary.
2. Front tyres under inflated.	2. Inflate tyres to correct pressures.
3. Incorrect tyres fitted.	3. Fit tyres of correct specification.
4. Seized steering ball joints and linkage.	4. Check components for wear and renew as necessary.
5. Seized front hub assembly components.	5. Check components for wear and renew as necessary.
6. Seized or worn steering box internal components.	6. Check components and renew as necessary.
7. Steering column intermediate shaft universal joint stiff or seized.	7. Inspect universal joints and lubricate if joints are okay. Renew intermediate shaft if universal joint is badly seized.
8. Steering column bearings or universal joint stiff or seized.	8. Inspect universal joint and lubricate if joint is okay. If universal joint is okay this would indicate seized column bearings. Renew steering column.

Excessive Power Steering System Noise

Possible Cause	Remedy
1. Incorrect fluid level in oil reservoir.	1. Top up or drain fluid to correct level and bleed PAS system.
2. High pressure hose in foul condition with chassis or body.	2. Check that hose is correctly routed and secured.
3. Insufficient lock angle,giving squeal on full lock.	3. Adjust steering lock to correct position.
4. Air in the PAS system,giving a continuous moan.	4. Bleed the PAS system.
5. Seized steering pump bearings.	5. Renew pump.
6. Start up noise from PAS in excessive cold climate.	6. Use optional Cold Climate PAS Fluid.

Dialogue

At the Auto Beauty Shop

（C：Customer　T：Technician）

T: Good afternoon, Madam. Is there anything I can help you with?

C: Oh, I bought a car ten days ago. This is the first time that I have come to your shop. What kinds of service do you offer?

T: We offer car washing (by hand or by machine) and waxing. Common maintenance of cars is also offered here. And we have various kinds of interior ornaments for customers to choose.

C: Do you guarantee quality?

T: Don't worry about it, Madam. All our workers are experts in washing, waxing and common maintenance of cars. The materials used and the interior ornaments offered are of high quality.

C: Generally, how often should a car be washed?

T: Cars should be washed once every month at least. During the washing, pressure water is used to remove the dirt from all the area where dirt and salt may be accumulated.

C: How about waxing?

T: You'd better have your car waxed at least once three or four month. Waxing helps to protect the pain from sun and chemicals. Besides, it can make your car look shiny.

C: How long will it take?

T: It will take you at least half an hour to have the whole car waxed. But the high quality car wax can stay on your car for three or four months.

C: Oh, I'm afraid I don't have much time to have my car waxed today. I'll come when I'm free. Now, just have my car washed, please.

T: OK. A complete clean up?

C: No, just exterior, please.

T: Washing by hand or by machine?

C: I think a hand wash will do. When will it be ready?

T: In about fifteen minutes.

C: How much should I pay?

T: Fifteen Yuan…

Automobile Brake System

Aims and Requirements

- List the components of a typical brake system
- Explain how a break system works
- Describe the structure of disk brake
- Describe the structure of drum brake
- List the anti-lock brake types
- Explain how an ABS works
- Translate the workshop manual
- Practice dialogues
- Cultivate students' awareness of environmental protection
- Cultivate students' information processing ability

Know the Structure

注释

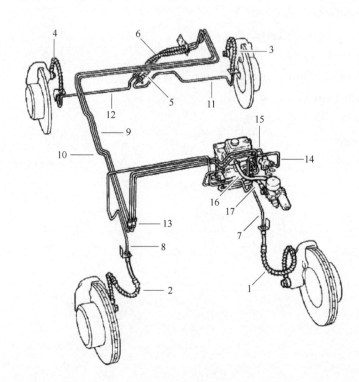

Fig. 8-1   Brake Pipe Layout

1. Front left hand	
2. Front right hand	
3. Rear left hand	
4. Rear right hand	
5. Rear left hand intermediate	
6. Rear right hand intermediate	
7. Feed to front left hand	
8. Feed to front right hand	
9. Feed to rear left hand intermediate hose	
10. Feed to rear right hand intermediate hose	
11. Feed to rear left hand flexible hose	
12. Feed to rear right hand flexible hose	
13. Two way connectors	
14. From PCRV	
15. To PCRV	
16. Fluid feed to pump	
17. Pressure fluid from pump	

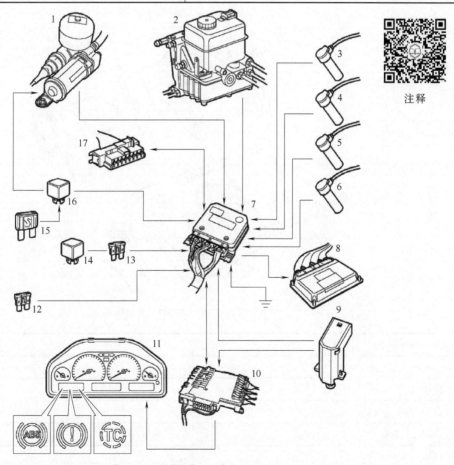

Fig. 8-2   ABS Control System

1. ABS power unit	
2. Brake booster/ABS modulator unit	
3. Front left speed sensor	
4. Front right speed sensor	
5. Rear left speed sensor	
6. Rear right speed sensor	
7. ABS ECU	
8. Engine Control Module	
9. Brake pedal switch	
10. Body electrical control module	
11. Instrument pack	
12. Fuse-Battery supply	
13. Fuse-Ignition supply	
14. Ignition relay	
15. Fuse-ABS power unit relay supply	
16. ABS power unit relay	
17. Diagnostic socket	

注释

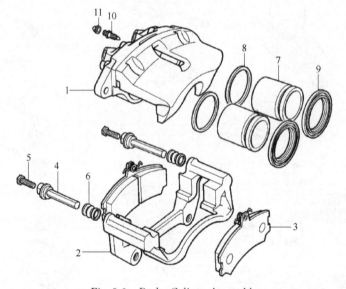

Fig. 8-3　Brake Caliper Assembly

1. Hydraulic body	
2. Carrier	
3. Brake pad	
4. Guide pin	
5. Guide pin bolt	
6. Guide pin boot	

续表

7. Piston	
8. Fluid seal	
9. Dust cover	
10. Bleed screw	
11. Dust cap	

Text A　Brake System

The modern automotive brake system has been refined for over 100 years and has become extremely dependable and efficient. The typical brake system consists of disk brakes in front and either disk or drum brakes in the rear connected by a system of tubes and hoses that link the brake at each wheel to the master cylinder, seeing Fig. 8-4. Other systems that are connected with the brake system include the parking brakes, power brake booster and the anti-lock system.

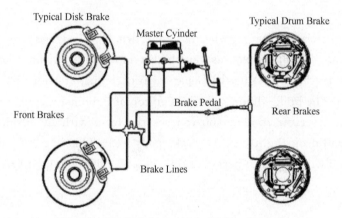

Fig. 8-4　Typical Automotive Braking System

How Brakes Work

When you step on the brake pedal, you are actually pushing against a plunger in the master cylinder, which forces hydraulic oil (brake fluid) through a series of tubes and hoses to the braking unit at each wheel. Since hydraulic fluid cannot be compressed, pushing fluid through a pipe is just like pushing a steel bar through a pipe. Unlike a steel bar, however, fluid can be directed through many twists and turns on its way to its destination, arriving with the exact same motion and pressure that it started with. On a disk brake, the fluid from the master cylinder is forced into a caliper where it presses against a piston[1]. The piston, in turn, squeezes two brake pads against the disk, which is attached to the wheel, forcing it to slow down or stop[2]. This process is similar to a bicycle brake where two rubber pads rub against the wheel rim creating friction.

With drum brakes, fluid is forced into the wheel cylinder, which pushes the brake shoes out so that the friction linings are pressed against the drum, which is attached to the wheel, causing the wheel to stop. In either case, the friction surfaces of the pads on a disk brake system, or the shoes on a drum brake convert the forward motion of the vehicle into heat. Heat is what causes the friction surfaces (linings) of the pads and shoes to eventually wear out and require replacement.

Master Cylinder

The master cylinder is located in the engine compartment on the firewall, directly in front of the driver's seat. A typical master cylinder has actually two completely separate master cylinders in one housing, each handling two wheels. In this way if one side fails, you will still be able to stop the car. The brake warning light on the dash will light if either side fails, alerting you to the problem[3] . Master cylinders have become very reliable and rarely malfunction. However, the most common problem that they experience is an internal leak. This will cause the brake pedal to slowly sink to the floor when your foot applies steady pressure.

Brake Fluid

Brake fluid is special oil that has specific properties. It is designed to withstand cold temperatures without thickening as well as very high temperatures without boiling. Brake fluid must meet standards that are set by the Department of Transportation (DOT) . The current standard is DOT-3. The brake fluid reservoir is on top of the master cylinder. Most cars today have a transparent reservoir so that you can see the level without opening the cover. The brake fluid level will drop slightly as the brake pads wear. This is a normal condition. If the level drops noticeably over a short period of time or goes down to about two thirds full, have your brakes checked as soon as possible[4] .

Brake Lines

The brake fluid travels from the master cylinder to the wheels through a series of steel tubes and reinforced rubber hoses. Rubber hoses are used only in places that require flexibility, such as at the front wheels, which move up and down as well as steer.

Disk Brakes

The disk brake is the best brake we have found so far. Disk brakes are used to stop everything from cars to locomotives and jumbo jets. Disk brakes wear longer, and are less affected by water, and are self-adjusting and self-cleaning. The main components of a disk brake are the brake pads, rotor, caliper and caliper support, seeing Fig. 8-5.

Brake Pads

There are two brake pads on each caliper. They are constructed of a metal "shoe" with the lining riveted or bonded to it. The pads are mounted in the caliper, one on each side of the rotor. Brake linings used to be made primarily of asbestos because of its heat absorbing properties and quiet operation. However, due to health risks, asbestos has been outlawed, so new materials are now being used. Brake pads wear out with use and must be replaced periodically. There are many types and qualities of pads available. The differences have to do with brake life (how long the new pads will last) and noise (how quiet they are when you step on the brake). Harder linings tend to last longer and stop better under heavy use but they may produce an irritating squeal when they are applied. Technicians that work on brakes usually have a favorite pad that gives a good compromise that their customers can live with.

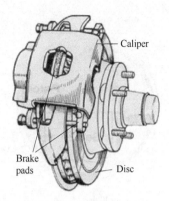

Fig. 8-5　Disk Brake of ChangAn Vehicle

Rotor

The disk rotor is made of iron with highly machined surfaces where the brake pads contact it. Just as the brake pads wear out over time, the rotor also undergoes some wear, usually in the form of ridges and grooves where the brake pad rubs against it. This wear pattern exactly matches the wear pattern of the pads as they seat themselves to the rotor. When the pads are replaced, the rotor must be machined smooth to allow the new pads to have an even contact surface to work with. Only a small amount of material can be machined off of a rotor before it becomes unusable and must be replaced.

Caliper and Support

There are two main types of calipers: Floating calipers and fixed calipers. There are other configurations but these are the most popular. Calipers must be replaced if they show signs of leaking brake fluid.

Single piston floating calipers are the most popular and also least costly to manufacture and service. A floating caliper "floats" or moves in a track in its support so that it can center itself over the rotor. As you apply brake pressure, the hydraulic fluid pushes in two directions. It forces the piston against the inner pad, which in turn pushes against the rotor. It also pushes the caliper in the opposite direction against the outer pad, pressing it against the other side of the rotor. Floating calipers are also available on some vehicles with two pistons mounted on the same side. Two piston floating calipers are found on more expensive cars and can provide an improved braking "feel".

Four piston fixed calipers are mounted rigidly to the support and are not allowed to move. Instead, there are two pistons on each side that press the pads against the rotor. Four piston calipers have a better feel and are more efficient, but are more expensive to produce and cost more to service. This type of caliper is usually found on more expensive luxury and high performance cars.

Drum Brakes

Most vehicles produced for many years have disk brakes on the front; drum brakes are

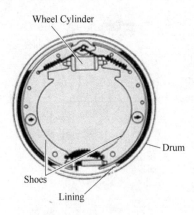

Fig. 8-6 Drum Brake

cheaper to produce for the rear wheels, seeing Fig. 8-6. The main reason is the parking brake system. On drum brakes, adding a parking brake is the simple addition of a lever, while on disk brakes, we need a complete mechanism, in some cases, a complete mechanical drum brake assembly inside the disk brake rotor. Parking brakes must be a separate system that does not use hydraulics. Drum brakes consist of a backing plate, brake shoes, brake drum, wheel cylinder, return springs and an automatic or self-adjusting system. When you apply the brakes, brake fluid is forced under pressure into the wheel cylinder, which in turn pushes the brake shoes into contact with the machined surface on the inside of the drum. When the pressure is released, return springs pull the shoes back to their rest position. As the brake linings wear, the shoes must travel a greater distance to reach the drum. When the distance reaches a certain point, a self-adjusting mechanism automatically reacts by adjusting the rest position of the shoes so that they are closer to the drum.

Power Brake Booster

The power brake booster is mounted on the firewall directly behind the master cylinder, along with the master cylinder, is directly connected with the brake pedal. Its purpose is to amplify the available foot pressure applied to the brake pedal so that the amount of foot pressure required to stop even the largest vehicle is minimal. Power for the booster comes from engine vacuum. The automobile engine produces vacuum as a by-product of normal operation and is freely available for use in powering accessories such as the power brake booster. Vacuum enters the booster through a check valve on the booster. The check valve is connected to the engine with a rubber hose and acts as a one-way valve that allows vacuum to enter the booster but does not let it escape. The booster is an empty shell that is divided into two chambers by a rubber diaphragm[5] . There is a valve in the diaphragm that remains open while your foot is off the brake pedal so that vacuum is allowed to fill both chambers. When you step on the brake pedal, the valve in the diaphragm closes, separating the two chambers and another valve opens to allow air in the chamber on the brake pedal side. This is what provides the power assist. In order to have power assist, the engine must be running. If the engine stalls or shuts off while you are driving, you will have a small reserve of power assist for two or three pedal applications, after that, the brakes will be extremely hard to apply and you must put as much pressure as you can to bring the vehicle to a stop.

New Words

refine   [ri'fain]   *vt.* 精炼，精制，精选，改进

dependable	[di'pendəbl]	*adj.* 可靠的，可信的
plunger	['plʌndʒə]	*n.* 活塞，柱塞
destination	[desti'neiʃən]	*n.* 目的地，终点
rim	[rim]	*n.* 边缘，边沿，胎环
lining	['lainiŋ]	*n.* 衬片，衬垫
eventually	[i'ventjuəli]	*adv.* 最后，终于
reliable	[ri'laiəbl]	*adj.* 可靠的，安全的
malfunction	[mæl'fʌŋkʃən]	*n.* 不正常起动，故障，出错
steady	['stedi]	*adj.* 稳定的，平稳的，持续的
property	['prɔpəti]	*n.* 性能，特性
transparent	[træns'pɛərent]	*adj.* 透明的，半透明的
noticeably	['nəutisəbli]	*adv.* 易见地，显著地
flexibility	[fleksə'biliti]	*n.* 柔韧，易弯曲，弹性
caliper	['kælipə]	*n.* 碟形制动器
bond	[bɔnd]	*vt.* 焊接，粘接
asbestos	[æz'bestəs]	*n.* 石棉
irritating	['iriteitiŋ]	*adj.* 刺激的
squeal	[skwi:l]	*n.* 尖叫声，振鸣声
technician	[tek'niʃən]	*n.* 技术人员
ridge	[ridʒ]	*n.* 背脊，峰，隆起线
unusable	[ʌn'ju:zəbl]	*adj.* 不可用的，不能使用的
amplify	['æmplifai]	*vt.* 增强，加强，扩大

Phrases and Expressions

disk brake	盘式制动器，碟刹
drum brake	鼓式制动器
parking brake	驻车制动
power brake booster	真空助力器
brake pedal	制动踏板
master cylinder	主缸
brake fluid	制动液，刹车油
brake pad	制动快，制动衬垫
so far	迄今，至今
wear out	磨损，用坏，用旧
one-way valve	单向阀

Notes to the Text

[1]　On a disk brake，the fluid from the master cylinder is forced into a caliper where it presses against a piston.

碟刹时，运用刹车总泵输送来的刹车油压送到制动钳，制动钳推动活塞。　　音频讲解 [1]

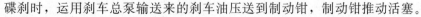

〔2〕 The piston, in turn, squeezes two brake pads against the disk, which is attached to the wheel, forcing it to slow down or stop.

依次，活塞挤压制动钳上的两个摩擦片，推动摩擦片压向固定在车轮上的制动盘，迫使汽车减速或停下来。

〔3〕 The brake warning light on the dash will light if either side fails, alerting you to the problem.

如果一侧出现故障，仪表盘上的刹车警示灯就会亮起，提示您刹车系统可能出现问题。

〔4〕 If the level drops noticeably over a short period of time or goes down to about two thirds full, have your brakes checked as soon as possible.

如果在短时间内刹车液的液位下降明显或下降到三分之二，请尽快检查你的刹车盘。

〔5〕 The booster is an empty shell that is divided into two chambers by a rubber diaphragm.

助力器是一个腔体，内部有一个橡胶膜片将腔体隔成两部分。

Exercises

1. Answer the following questions according to the text

(1) How do brakes work?

(2) Do you know how a bicycle brake works?

(3) Where is the master cylinder?

(4) Why does a typical master cylinder have two completely separate master cylinders?

(5) Is brake fluid special oil? List the reasons.

(6) How will you do if calipers show signs of leaking brake fluid?

(7) Why do most vehicles have disk brakes on the front and drum brakes for the rear wheels?

(8) What will you do if the engine stalls while you are driving?

2. Translate the following into Chinese

(1) hydraulic braking system

(2) brake pedal

(3) master cylinder

(4) wheel cylinder

(5) brake lining

(6) brake rotor

(7) booster control valve

(8) one-way valve

3. Translate the following into English

(1) 刹车开关

(2) 空挡位置

(3) 制动距离

（4）驻车制动系统

（5）制动液

（6）碟式刹车

（7）刹车蹄片

（8）鼓式刹车

4. Fill in the blanks with the words or phrases given below，change the form where necessary

divide into	along with	so far	wear out
push against	just like	due to	such as

（1）When you step on the brake pedal，you are actually _____ a plunger in the master cylinder，which forces hydraulic oil through a series of tubes and hoses to the braking unit at each wheel.

（2）Since hydraulic fluid cannot be compressed，pushing hydraulic fluid through a pipe is _____ pushing a steel bar through a pipe.

（3）Rubber hoses are used only in places that require flexibility，_____ at the front wheels，which move up and down as well as steer.

（4）The disk brake is the best brake we have found _____ .

（5）However，_____ health risks，asbestos has been outlawed，so new materials are now being used.

（6）Brake pads _____ with use and must be replaced periodically.

（7）The power brake booster is mounted on the firewall directly behind the master cylinder，_____ the master cylinder，is directly connected with the brake pedal.

（8）The booster is an empty shell that is _____ two chambers by a rubber diaphragm.

Text B　Anti-lock Brake System

Stopping a car in a hurry on a slippery road can be very challenging. Anti-lock braking systems（ABS）take a lot of the challenge out of this event. In fact，on slippery surfaces，even professional drivers can't stop as quickly without ABS as an average driver can with ABS[1] .

The ABS System

The theory behind anti-lock brakes is simple. A skidding wheel（where the tire contact patch is sliding relative to the road）has less traction than a non-skidding wheel. If you have been stuck on ice，you know that if your wheels are spinning you have no traction. This is because the contact patch is sliding relative to the ice. By keeping the wheels from skidding while you slow down，anti-lock brakes benefit you in two ways：You'll stop faster，and you'll be able to steer while you stop. There are four main components to an ABS system：speed sensors，pump，valves and controller，seeing Fig. 8-7.

Speed Sensors

The anti-lock braking system needs some way of knowing when a wheel is about to lock up. The speed sensors, which are located at each wheel, or in some cases in the differential, provide this information.

Valves

There is a valve in the brake line of each brake controlled by the ABS. On some systems, the valve has three positions:

In position one, the valve is open. Pressure from the master cylinder is passed right through to the brake.

In position two, the valve blocks the line, isolating that brake from the master cylinder. This prevents the pressure from rising further should the driver push the brake pedal harder[2].

In position three, the valve releases some of the pressure from the brake.

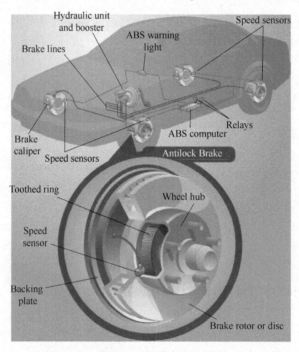

Fig. 8-7　Anti-lock Brake Components

Fig. 8-8　Anti-lock Brake Pump and Valves

Pump

Since the valve is able to release pressure from the brakes, there has to be some way to put that pressure back. That is what the pump does. When a valve reduces the pressure in a line, the pump is there to get the pressure back up, seeing Fig. 8-8.

Controller

The controller is a computer in the car. It watches the speed sensors and controls the valves.

ABS at Work

There are many different variations and control algorithms for ABS systems. We will discuss how one of the simpler systems works.

The controller monitors the speed sensors at all times. It is looking for decelerations in the wheel that are out of the ordinary. Right before a wheel locks up, it will experience a rapid deceleration. It might take a car five seconds to stop from 60mph (96. 6kph) under ideal conditions, but a wheel that locks up could stop spinning in less than a second[3] .

The ABS controller knows that such a rapid deceleration is impossible, so it reduces the pressure to that brake until it sees an acceleration, then it increases the pressure until it sees the deceleration again[4] . It can do this very quickly, before the tire can actually significantly change speed. The result is that the tire slows down at the same rate as the car, with the brakes keeping the tires very near the point at which they will start to lock up[5] . This gives the system maximum braking power.

When the ABS system is in operation you will feel a pulsing in the brake pedal, this comes from the rapid opening and closing of the valves. Some ABS systems can cycle up to 15 times per second.

Anti-Lock Brake Types

Anti-lock braking systems use different schemes depending on the type of brakes in use. We will refer to them by the number of channels (that is, how many valves that are individually controlled) and the number of speed sensors.

Four-channel, Four-sensor ABS

This is the best scheme. There is a speed sensor on all four wheels and a separate valve for all four wheels. With this setup, the controller monitors each wheel individually to make sure it is achieving maximum braking force.

Three-channel, Three-sensor ABS

This scheme, commonly found on pickup trucks with four-wheel ABS, has a speed sensor and a valve for each of the front wheels, with one valve and one sensor for both rear wheels[6] . The speed sensor for the rear wheels is located in the rear axle.

This system provides individual control of the front wheels, so they can both achieve maximum braking force. The rear wheels, however, are monitored together, they both have to start to lock up before the ABS will activate on the rear. With this system, it is possible that one of the rear wheels will lock during a stop, reducing brake effectiveness.

One-channel, One-sensor ABS

This system is commonly found on pickup trucks with rear-wheel ABS. It has one valve, which controls both rear wheels, and one speed sensor, located in the rear axle.

This system operates the same as the rear end of a three-channel system. The rear wheels are monitored together and they both have to start to lock up before the ABS kicks in. In this system it is also possible that one of the rear wheels will lock, reducing brake effectiveness.

This system is easy to identify. Usually there will be one brake line going through a T-fitting to both rear wheels. You can locate the speed sensor by looking for an electrical connection near the differential on the rear-axle housing.

New Words

slippery	[slipəri]	adj. 滑的，光滑的
skidding	[skidiŋ]	adj. 滑动的，滑溜的，打滑的
controller	[kən'trəulə]	n. 控制器，调节器，擦纵器
isolate	['aisəleit]	vt. 分离，断开
deceleration	[di:selə'reiʃən]	n. 减速，熄灭
ordinary	['ɔ:dinəri]	adj. 正常的，规定的
scheme	[ski:m]	n. 设计图，方案，系统

Phrases and Expressions

in a hurry	匆忙
anti-lock brake system	防抱死制动系统
speed sensor	速度传感器
be about to	即将
at all times	无论何时，一直
lock up	闭锁，锁住，固定
in operation	操作中，运转中
in use	在使用着
refer to	谈到，涉及，查询，参考
rear-axle housing	后桥壳，后轴壳

Notes to the Text

[1]　In fact, on slippery surfaces, even professional drivers can't stop as quickly without ABS as an average driver can with ABS.

事实上，在湿滑路面上对于没装防抱死制动系统的车辆，即使是职业司机也没有一般人驾驶的装了防抱死制动系统的车辆刹车快。

音频讲解 [1]

[2]　This prevents the pressure from rising further should the driver push the brake pedal harder.

即使驾驶员用较大的力踩下制动踏板，也可以阻挡压力进一步增加。

音频讲解 [2]

[3]　It might take a car five seconds to stop from 60mph (96.6kph) under ideal conditions, but a wheel that locks up could stop spinning in less than a second.

在理想状况下，一辆汽车可能需要用 5 秒时间从 60 英里/小时（96.6 公里/小时）的速度下停下来，然而被锁死的轮胎不到一秒钟就不能转动了。

音频讲解 [3]

[4]　The ABS controller knows that such a rapid deceleration is impossible, so it reduces the pressure to that brake until it sees an acceleration,

then it increases the pressure until it sees the deceleration again.

防抱死制动系统控制器清楚这样快地减速是不可能的，所以，降低该车轮的制动力，车轮又继续转动，转动到一定程度，控制器再施加制动力，车轮又减速。

音频讲解 [4]

［5］ The result is that the tire slows down at the same rate as the car, with the brakes keeping the tires very near the point at which they will start to lock up.

结果是轮胎以相同的速率减速，车轮既受制动又避过即将到达的下一个锁死点。

音频讲解 [5]

［6］ This scheme，commonly found on pickup trucks with four-wheel ABS，has a speed sensor and a valve for each of the front wheels，with one valve and one sensor for both rear wheels.

这种系统普遍存在于装有四轮防抱死制动系统的小吨位货车上，两前轮各有一个轮速传感器和电磁阀，而两后轮共用一个轮速传感器和电磁阀。

音频讲解 [6]

Exercises

1. Translate the following abbreviations into corresponding Chinese terms

（1）BMC（brake master cylinder）

（2）PKB（parking brake）

（3）ABS（anti-lock brake system）

（4）EBD（electronic brakeforce distribution）

（5）CBC（cornering brake control）

（6）ASR（acceleration slip regulation）

（7）BPM（brake pressure modulator）

（8）BA（brake assist）

2. Translate the following sentences into Chinese

（1）Stopping a car in a hurry on a slippery road can be very challenging.

（2）There are four main components to an ABS system：speed sensors，pump，valves and controller.

（3）The speed sensors，which are located at each wheel，or in some cases in the differential，provide this information.

（4）Since the valve is able to release pressure from the brakes，there has to be some way to put that pressure back.

（5）When the ABS system is in operation you will feel a pulsing in the brake pedal，this comes from the rapid opening and closing of the valves.

（6）Anti-lock braking systems use different schemes depending on the type of brakes in use.

（7）This system provides individual control of the front wheels，so they can both achieve maximum braking force.

（8）In this system it is also possible that one of the rear wheels will lock，reducing brake effectiveness.

Workshop Manual

ABS Electronic Control Unit

ABS/ETC operation is controlled by the ECU. The ECU is attached to a bracket which in turn is attached to the bulkhead.

The ECU is connected to the ABS harness by a 35 pin connector on up to 99MY vehicles and by 9，15 and 18 pin connectors on vehicles from 99MY.

When system faults are detected by the ECU，warning lamps in the instrument pack can be illuminated for ABS，ETC and braking system faults. Certain faults are also displayed in the instrument pack message centre.

The ABS ECU generates a digital road speed signal from the average speed of the four wheels. The ABS ECU passes the road speed signal to the BECM. The BECM outputs the road speed signal to the following interfaces：

—Engine control module (ECM) .

—Cruise control ECU.

—Instrument pack.

—Air temperature control (ATC) ECU.

—In-car entertainment (ICE) .

—Electronic air suspension (EAS) ECU.

—Electronic automatic transmission (EAT) ECU.

The ABS ECU also outputs a rough road signal to the ECM on V8 engine vehicles only. The digital rough road signal is generated from the difference in rotational speed of each wheel.

The ECU is a non-serviceable item. It must be replaced if failure occurs.

Brake Warning Lamp

The warning lamp situated in instrument binnacle indicates insufficient pressure in system and/or low fluid level and/or park brake applied. The warning lamp will illuminate，for 3 seconds when ignition is switched on as part of initial bulb check，and continuously when parking brake is applied. If the pressure in hydraulic system is lower than the cut-in pressure for the warning lamp，the lamp will illuminate. When the lamp is on hydraulic pump will be heard running.

The ABS warning lamp situated in instrument binnacle indicates a failure in ABS system.

The warning lamp will illuminate for 1 second when ignition is switched on，it will briefly extinguish and will illuminate again. This indicates that the system self monitoring check was successful，and system performs correctly.

If it does not extinguish and illuminate again a system fault has occurred. The warning lamp will extinguish when vehicle speed exceeds 7km/h (5mph) .

If lamp remains on or subsequently illuminates a fault in ABS system is indicated. The self monitoring procedure is repeated frequently while ignition is on. If a fault is detected during self monitoring, the lamp will illuminate indicating that one or more wheels are not under ABS control.

Dialogue

Auto Beauty

(C: Customer   T: Technician)

T: Hello. This is Army's Auto Beauty Shop. Can I help you?

C: This is Bruce. I think my car want to be cleaned and waxed. Can you come to pick up my car?

T: Certainly. Can you tell me where you live? I'll pick up your car in half an hour.

C: My house is at No. 16 Hong Kong road. How much is a complete clean-up please?

T: Five hundred Yuan including materials and labor.

C: I think it needs a hand wash.

T: Exterior and interior?

C: Exterior, please. It looks okay inside. We just cleaned the seat last week.

T: Will you come to pick it up, or shall we drive it to your place?

C: Deliver it to Bruce office, please. When will it be ready?

T: About 2 o'clock this afternoon.

C: How much should I pay?

T: One hundred and fifteen Yuan. You need not pay now. Pay when you get the car.

Automobile Body Electrical System

Aims and Requirements

- Explain how power door locks work
- List the ways to unlock car doors
- Describe the functions of window lifting mechanism
- Explain the circuit of power window
- List the types of wiper blade scheme
- Translate the workshop manual
- Practice dialogues
- Strictly follow the automobile maintenance industry standards
- Cultivate students' teamwork spirit

Know the Structure

注释

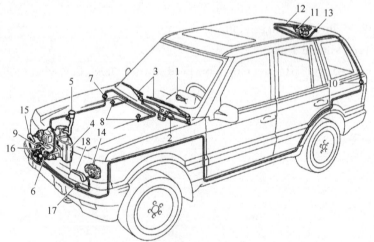

Fig. 9-1   Wiper and Washer System

1. Multi-switch	
2. Wiper motor, windscreen	
3. Wiper arm/blade	
4. Washer reservoir	
5. Filler cap tube, washer reservoir	

续表

6. Windscreen washer pump	
7. Non return valve	
8. Washer jets	
9. Rear screen washer pump	
10. Non return valve	
11. Wiper motor, rear screen	
12. Wiper arm/blade	
13. Washer jet	
14. Wiper motor, headlamp	
15. Wiper arm/blade	
16. Washer pump, headlamp	
17. Non return valve	
18. Washer jet	

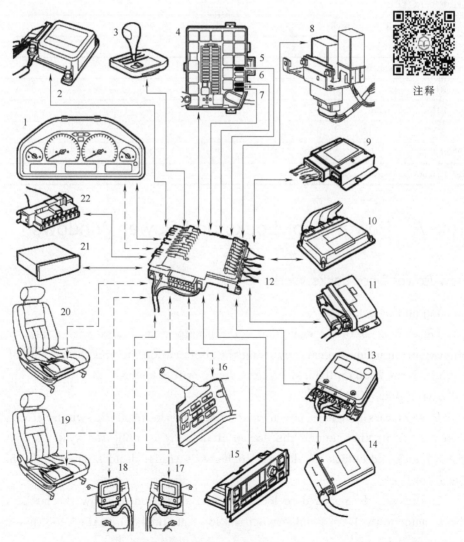

注释

Fig. 9-2   BECM Control Schematics

1. Instrument pack	
2. SRS diagnostic control unit (DCU)	
3. Selector lever	
4. Engine compartment fusebox	
5. Maxi fuse 1-Power supply	
6. Maxi fuse 4-Power supply	
7. Maxi fuse 5-Power supply	
8. Cruise control ECU	
9. Transfer box ECU	
10. Engine control module (ECM)	
11. Electronic automatic transmission (EAT) ECU	
12. ABS ECU	
13. Electronic air suspension (EAS) ECU	
14. HEVAC ECU	
15. Centre console switch pack	
16. RH door outstation	
17. LH door outstation	
18. RH seat outstation	
19. LH seat outstation	
20. BECM	
21. ICE unit	
22. Diagnostic socket	

Text A   Power Door Locks and Power Windows

How Power Door Locks Work

Locking and Unlocking

Here are some of the ways that you can unlock car doors: with a key, by pressing the unlock button inside the car, by using the combination lock on the outside of the door, by pulling up the knob on the inside of the door, with a keyless-entry remote control, by a signal from a control center.

In some cars that have power door locks, the lock-unlock switch actually sends power to the actuators that unlock the door. But in more complicated systems that have several ways to lock and unlock the doors, the body controller decides when to do the unlocking.

Car Door Lock

In the car, the power-door-lock actuator is positioned below the latch. A rod connects the actuator to the latch, and another rod connects the latch to the knob that sticks up out of the top of the door[1].

When the actuator moves the latch up, it connects the outside door handle to the opening mechanism. When the latch is down, the outside door handle is disconnected from the mechanism so that it cannot be opened.

Actuator

The power-door-lock actuator can move the metal hook shown in Fig. 9-3 to the left or right. When mounted in the car, it is vertical, so the hook can move up or down. It mimics your motions when you pull the knob up or push it down.

Fig. 9-3 Power-door-lock Actuator of ChangHe Vehicle

Inside the power-door-lock actuator, a small electric motor turns a series of spur gears that serve as a gear reduction. The last gear drives a rack-and-pinion gear set that is connected to the actuator rod. The rack converts the rotational motion of the motor into the linear motion needed to move the lock.

How Power Windows Work

Lifting Mechanism

See Fig. 9-4, the window lift on most cars uses a really neat linkage to lift the window glass while keeping it level[2] . A small electric motor is attached to a worm gear and several other spur gears to create a large gear reduction, giving it enough torque to lift the window.

An important feature of power windows is that they cannot be forced open, the worm gear in the drive mechanism takes care of this. Many worm gears have a self-locking feature because of the angle of contact between the worm and the gear. The worm can spin the gear, but the gear cannot spin the worm, friction between the teeth causes the gears to bind.

Fig. 9-4 Window Lifting Mechanism

The linkage has a long arm, which attaches to a bar that holds the bottom of the window. The end of the arm can slide in a groove in the bar as the window rises. On the other end of the bar is a large plate that has gear teeth cut into it, and the motor turns a gear that engages these teeth.

The same linkage is often used on cars with manual windows, but instead of a motor turning the gear, the crank handle turns it.

Wiring and Switch

In Fig. 9-5, the power is fed to the driver's door through a 20A fuse. The power comes into the window-switch control panel on the door. Two contacts, one on either side of the power contact, are connected to the vehicle ground and to the motor[3] . The power also runs through the lockout switch to a similar window switch on each of the other doors.

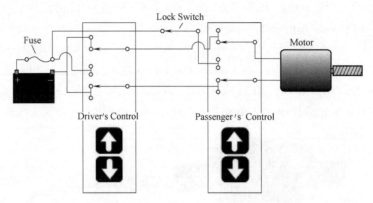

Fig. 9-5   A Simple Power Window Circuit

When the driver presses one of the switches，one of the two side contacts is disconnected from the ground and connected to the center power contact，while the other one remains grounded. This provides power to the window motor. If the switch is pressed the other way，then power runs through the motor in the opposite direction.

Some Advanced Systems

On some cars，the power windows work in a completely different way. Instead of the power for the motor going through the switches directly，the switches are connected to the driver's door module，as well as a central module called the body controller. The driver's door module monitors all of the switches. For instance，if the driver presses his window switch，the door module closes a relay that provides power to the window motor. If the driver presses the switch to adjust the passenger-side window，the driver's door module sends a packet of data onto the communication bus of the car[4]. This packet tells the body controller to energize one of the power window motors.

The automatic-down feature is fairly common on cars with power windows. You tap and release the down switch and the window goes all the way down. This feature uses a circuit that monitors the amount of time you hold the switch down. If the switch is down for less than about half a second，the window will go all the way down until it hits the limit switch. If you hold the switch down for longer than that，the window will stop when you release the button.

On the Volkswagen in the TV commercial，the windows can be lowered by inserting the key in the driver's door，turning and holding it. This feature is controlled by the driver's door module，which monitors a switch in the door lock. If the key is held turned for more than a set amount of time，the driver's door module lowers the windows.

New Words

knob	[nɔb]	n. 球形捏手，球形突出物，旋钮
remote	[ri'məut]	adj. 遥远的
actuator	['æktjueitə]	n. 执行机构，执行器

latch	[lætʃ]	n. 门插销
mimic	['mimik]	vt. 模仿，模拟
bind	[baind]	v. 绑，约束
communication	[kə,mjuːni'keiʃn]	n. 信息，通讯
energize	['enədʒaiz]	vt. 使活跃，给与……电压
tap	[tæp]	vt. 轻打，轻敲
lower	['ləuə]	vt. 放下，降下，减弱，贬低

Phrases and Expressions

power Door Lock	动力门锁
keyless-entry remote control	无钥匙强入系统
body controller	车身控制单元
stick up	竖起，突起
door handle	门把手
spur gear	直齿轮
power window	动力车窗
window-switch control panel	车窗开关控制面板
lockout switch	锁止开关
limit switch	限位开关

Notes to the Text

[1]　A rod connects the actuator to the latch，and another rod connects the latch to the knob that sticks up out of the top of the door.

执行器与门插销由一连杆相连，同时通过另一连杆与外漏在车门上端的球形捏手相连。

音频讲解 [1]

[2]　See Fig. 9-4，the window lift on most cars uses a really neat linkage to lift the window glass while keeping it level.

如图 9-4 所示，大多数汽车采用连杆机构举升车窗，并保持车窗水平。

音频讲解 [2]

[3]　Two contacts，one on either side of the power contact，are connected to the vehicle ground and to the motor.

位于电源触点两侧的两个触点均与车身搭铁和车窗电机相连。

[4]　If the driver presses the switch to adjust the passenger-side window，the driver's door module sends a packet of data onto the communication bus of the car.

音频讲解 [3]

如果驾驶员操纵开关调整乘员侧车窗，驾驶员侧车门模块会将这一信息发送到车载网络上。

Exercises

音频讲解 [4]

1. Answer the following questions according to the text

（1）How many ways can you list to unlock car doors？

（2）What is the power-door-lock actuator's function?

（3）What components does a power-door-lock contain?

（4）How does a power-door-lock actuator work?

（5）What is the function of window lifting mechanism?

（6）Why cannot the gear spin the worm?

（7）How does the door module control the passenger-side window?

（8）What is the automatic-down feature of power windows?

2. Translate the following into Chinese

（1）instead of

（2）door module

（3）for instance

（4）TV commercial

（5）a set amount of

（6）remote control

（7）control panel

（8）lifting mechanism

3. Translate the following into English

（1）动力门锁

（2）车身控制单元

（3）门把手

（4）直齿轮

（5）动力车窗

（6）锁止开关

（7）限位开关

（8）遥控门锁

4. Fill in the blanks with the words or phrases given below, change the form where necessary

come into	feed to	less than	all the way
attach to	move up	serve as	take care of

（1）When mounted in the car, it is vertical, so the hook can _____ or down.

（2）Inside the power-door-lock actuator, a small electric motor turns a series of spur gears that _____ a gear reduction.

（3）An important feature of power windows is that they cannot be forced open, the worm gear in the drive mechanism _____ this.

（4）The linkage has a long arm, which _____ a bar that holds the bottom of the window.

（5）The power is _____ the driver's door through a 20A fuse.

（6）The power _____ the window-switch control panel on the door.

（7）You tap and release the down switch and the window goes _____ down.

（8）If the switch is down for _____ about half a second, the window will go all the way down until it hits the limit switch.

Text B Windshield Wiper

The first windshield wipers were operated manually by moving a lever inside the car back and forth. Today, most of us take our electric windshield wipers for granted. The wipers faithfully keep the window clear, moving back and forth across the windshield countless times as they sweep the water away. On their highest speed, they move impressively fast, sometimes shaking the car from side to side. What kind of a mechanism can move the wiper arms so effectively and so reliably?

Inside the Windshield Wiper

See Fig. 9-6, the windshield wiper combines two mechanical technologies to perform their task:

A combination electric motor and worm gear reduction provides power to the wiper.

A neat linkage converts the rotational output of the motor into the back-and-forth motion of the wipers.

Motor and Gear Reduction

It takes a lot of force to accelerate the wiper blades back and forth across the windshield so quick-

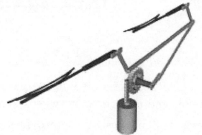

Fig. 9-6   A Windshield Wiper

ly. In order to generate this type of force, a worm gear is used on the output of a small electric motor.

The worm gear reduction can multiply the torque of the motor by about 50 times, while slowing the output speed of the electric motor by 50 times as well. The output of the gear reduction operates a linkage that moves the wipers back and forth.

Inside the motor and gear assembly is an electronic circuit that senses when the wipers are in their down position. The circuit maintains power to the wipers until they are parked at the bottom of the windshield, and then cuts the power to the motor. This circuit also parks the wipers between wipes when they are on their intermittent setting.

Linkage

A short rod is attached to the output shaft of the gear reduction. This rod spins around as the wiper motor turns. The short rod is connected to a long rod, as it spins, the long rod moves the rod back and forth. The long rod is connected to a rocker arm that actuates the wiper blade on the driver's side. Another long rod transmits the force from the driver-side to the passenger-side wiper blade.

Wiper Blade

Wiper blades are like squeegees. The arms of the wiper drag a thin rubber strip across the windshield to clear away the water.

Most cars have pretty much the same wiper design. Two blades move together to clean the windshield. One of the blades pivots from a point close to the driver's side of the car, and the other blade pivots from near the middle of the windshield. This is the tandem system, seeing Fig. 9-7. This design clears most of the windshield that is in the driver's field of view.

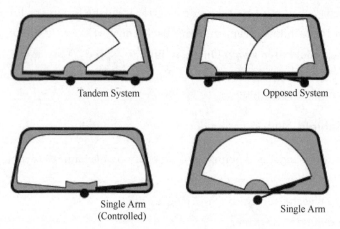

Fig. 9-7　Some of the Different Wiper Blade Schemes

There are a couple of other designs on some cars. Mercedes uses a single wiper arm that extends and retracts as it sweeps across the window, single arm (controlled) in the figure above[1] . This design also provides good coverage, but is more complicated than the standard dual-wiper systems. Some cars use wiper blades that are mounted on opposite sides of the windshield and move in the opposite direction, and some vehicles have a single wiper mounted in the middle. These systems don't provide as much coverage for the driver as the standard two-blade system.

Wiper Control

Most wipers have a low and a high speed, as well as an intermittent setting[2] . When the wipers are on low and high speed, the motor runs continuously. But in the intermittent setting, the wipers stop momentarily between each wipe. There are many different kinds of switches for wipers. Some cars have just one intermittent speed, others have 10 discrete settings and still others have a sliding scale that can be set for almost any time interval[3] .

Whichever kind of controls your car has, setting them just right can be tricky, too fast, the windshield gets dry and the wipers squeak, too slow, your visibility is blocked by raindrops. It can require almost constant attention to keep the wipers operating properly. Carmakers may finally have conquered this problem with the rain-sensing wiper.

Rain-sensing Wiper

In the past, automakers have tried to either eliminate the wipers or to control their speed automatically. However, a new type of wiper system is starting to appear on cars that actually do a good job of detecting the amount of water on the windshield and controlling the wipers. One such system is made by TRW limited company. The TRW system is found on many General Motors cars，including all Cadillac models.

The TRW system uses optical sensors to detect the moisture. The sensor is mounted in contact with the inside of the windshield，near the rearview mirror. The sensor projects infrared light into the windshield at a 45-degree angle. If the glass is dry，most of this light is reflected back into the sensor by the front of the windshield. If water droplets are on the glass，they reflect the light in different directions，the wetter the glass，the less light makes it back into the sensor[4]．

The electronics and software in the sensor turn on the wipers when the amount of light reflected onto the sensor decreases to a preset level. The software sets the speed of the wipers based on how fast the moisture builds up between wipes. It can operate the wipers at any speed. The system adjusts the speed as often as necessary to match with the rate of moisture accumulation.

New Words

grant	[grɑːnt]	vt. 同意，准予，承认
faithfully	['feiθfuli]	adv. 忠诚地，如实地，切实遵守地
countless	['kautlis]	adj. 无数的，数不尽的
wipe	[waip]	v. 擦，擦去 n. 擦，拭
intermittent	[ˌintə(ː)'mitənt]	adj. 间歇的，断断续续的
squeegee	['skwiːdʒiː]	n. 橡胶扫帚，橡胶滚轴
tandem	['tændəm]	adv. 一前一后
retract	[ri'trækt]	v. 缩回，缩进，收回
discrete	[dis'kriːt]	adj. 不连续的，离散的
squeak	[skwiːk]	n. 尖叫声；v. 发出尖叫声
visibility	[ˌvizi'biliti]	n. 可见度，能见度
conquer	['kɔŋkə]	vt. 征服，战胜，克服
detect	[di'tekt]	vt. 察觉，发觉，探测
optical	['ɔptikəl]	adj. 光学的
project	['prɔdʒekt]	n. 计划，方案；v. 设计，计划，发射
infrared	['infrə'red]	adj. 红外线的
reflect	[ri'flekt]	v. 反射，反映
droplet	['drɔplit]	n. 小滴
accumulation	[əkjuːmju'leiʃn]	n. 积聚，堆积物

Phrases and Expressions

windshield wiper	挡风玻璃刮雨器
wiper blade	雨刮片
electronic circuit	电子电路
clear away	清除，消失

time interval	时间间隔
optical sensor	光学传感器，光敏元件
rearview mirror	后视镜

Notes to the Text

音频讲解 [1]

[1]   Mercedes uses a single wiper arm that extends and retracts as it sweeps across the window, single arm (controlled) in the figure above.

梅赛德斯只采用了一个雨刮片，雨刮片扫过风挡时可以伸长和缩短，如上图中所示，可控制的单片雨刮。

音频讲解 [2]

[2]   Most wipers have a low and a high speed, as well as an intermittent setting.

大多数雨刮都有低速挡、高速挡和间歇挡。

[3]   Some cars have just one intermittent speed, others have 10 discrete settings and still others have a sliding scale that can be set for almost any time interval.

音频讲解 [3]

汽车雨刮通常只设一个间歇挡，但有些汽车的间歇挡有十个，还有一些汽车可以根据需要设置任意间隔的间歇挡。

[4]   If water droplets are on the glass, they reflect the light in different directions, the wetter the glass, the less light makes it back into the sensor.

如果雨滴聚集在玻璃上，将会使光线向不同的方向反射，玻璃越湿，反射回传感器的光线就越少。

音频讲解 [4]

Exercises

1. Translate the following abbreviations into corresponding Chinese terms

（1）RM（relay module）

（2）ANT（antenna）

（3）A/C（air conditioning）

（4）IPC（instrument panel cluster）

（5）RKE（remote keyless entry）

（6）GPS（global positioning system）

（7）SRS（supplemental restraint system）

（8）CAN（controller area network）

2. Translate the following sentences into Chinese

（1）A neat linkage converts the rotational output of the motor into the back-and-forth motion of the wipers.

（2）It takes a lot of force to accelerate the wiper blades back and forth across the windshield so quickly.

（3）The worm gear reduction can multiply the torque of the motor by about 50 times, while slowing the output speed of the electric motor by 50 times as well.

（4）Inside the motor and gear assembly is an electronic circuit that senses when the wipers are in their down position.

(5) Another long rod transmits the force from the driver-side to the passenger-side wiper blade.

(6) Whichever kind of controls your car has, setting them just right can be tricky, too fast, the windshield gets dry and the wipers squeak, too slow, your visibility is blocked by raindrops.

(7) The sensor is mounted in contact with the inside of the windshield, near the rear-view mirror.

(8) The system adjusts the speed as often as necessary to match with the rate of moisture accumulation.

Workshop Manual

Power Window Motor Removal

(1) Remove the rear view mirror mounting screws and then remove the rear view mirror. Disconnect the remote control connector.

(2) Remove the safety lock knob. Remove the screws from the door.

(3) Insert a screwdriver between the trim fasteners and door panel to pry it loose. Disconnect the connectors (power window motor, power window main switch, door lock actuator and outside mirror).

(4) Remove the door trim seal.

(5) Detach the regulator assembly.

(6) Disconnect the power window motor from the regulator assembly.

Windshield Wiper System

The windshield wiper system is one of the most important safety factors on any piece of equipment. A typical electric windshield wiper system consists of a switch, motor assembly, wiper linkage and arms, and wiper blades. The description of the components is as follows.

The windshield wiper switch is a multi-position switch, which may contain a rheostat. Each switch position provides for different wiping speeds. The rheostat, if provided, operates the delay mode for a slow wiping action. This permits the operator to select a delayed wipe from every 3 to 20 seconds. A relay is frequently used to complete the circuit between the battery voltage and the wiper motor.

The wiper motor assembly operates on one, two, or three speeds. The motor has a worm gear on the armature shaft that drives one or two gears, and, in turn, operates the linkage to the wiper arms. The motor is a small, DC motor. Resistors are placed in the control circuit from the switch to reduce the current and provide different operating speeds.

The wiper linkage and arms transfer motion from the wiper motor transmission to the wiper blades. The rubber wiper blades fit on the wiper arms.

The wiper blade is a flexible rubber squeegee-type device. It may be steel or plastic backed and is designed to maintain total contact with the windshield throughout the stroke. Wiper blades should be inspected periodically. If they are hardened，cut，or split，they are to be replaced.

When electrical problems occur in the windshield wiper system，use the service manual and its wiring diagram of the circuit. First check the fuses，electrical connections，and all grounds. Then proceed with checking the components.

Dialogue

Insurance for a Family Car

(C：Customer   S：Salesman)

S：Good morning，sir. Can I help you?

C：I'm looking for insurance from your company. May I ask you a few questions about insurance?

S：Certainly. Go ahead，please.

C：Generally speaking，what risks the automobile must be covered?

S：Is you insurance aiming for a family car or a business car?

C：For a family car.

S：For a family car，it always covers vehicle loss，person in vehicle，the third party insurance，risk of breakage and insurance against theft，etc.

C：Generally，what risk will be covered for customers?

S：It is generally divided into two types：one is called all-risk；the other type is that customers can choose some of the risks according to their own requirements.

C：An all-risk policy covers every sort of hazard，doesn't it?

S：That's right. If your car is a new one，all-risk is a sensible choice.

C：Why?

S：Car troubles always seem to happen at the worst possible time. You can't always prevent disasters，but you can insure against them. Protect yourself and your family with an all-risk for your car，so that large expenses can't hit you at once.

C：OK. I'll take it. Thanks for your advice.

S：You are welcome.

Vocabulary

accomplished	[ə'kɔmpliʃt]	adj. 完成的，熟练的，多才多艺的
accordingly	[ə'kɔːdiŋli]	adv. 因此，从而
accumulation	[əkjuːmju'leiʃn]	n. 积聚，堆积物
activate	['æktiveit]	vt. 刺激，使活动；vi. 有活力
actuate	['æktjueit]	vt. 开动，促使
actuator	['æktjueitə]	n. 执行机构，执行器
additive	['æditiv]	adj. 附加的，添加的；n. 添加剂
adequate	['ædikwit]	adj. 适当的，足够的
advent	['ædvənt]	n. 出现，到来
algorithm	['ælgəriðəm]	n. 运算法则
alternative	[ɔːl'təːnətiv]	adj. 选择性的，二者择一的
alternator	['ɔːltə(ː)neitə]	n. 交流发电机
ammeter	['æmitə]	n. 电表
amplify	['æmplifai]	vt. 增强，加强，扩大
anticipation	[ˌæntisi'peiʃən]	n. 预期，预料
antifreeze	['ænti'friːz]	n. 防冻剂
appropriate	[ə'prəupriit]	adj. 适当的
approximately	[əprɔksi'mətli]	adv. 近似地，大约
armature	['ɑːmətjuə]	n. 电枢
asbestos	[æz'bestəs]	n. 石棉
assembly	[ə'sembli]	n. 部件，组件，集合，装配
atomize	['ætəmaiz]	vt. 将……喷成雾状
baffle	['bæfl]	vt. 困惑，阻碍，为难
bind	[baind]	v. 绑，约束
blade	[bleid]	n. 刀片，叶片
blend	[blend]	vt. 混合；n. 混合物
blow	[bləu]	v. 风吹，吹气于
blower	['bləuə]	n. 送风机，吹风机
bond	[bɔnd]	vt. 焊接，粘接
brass	[brɑːs]	n. 黄铜，黄铜制品
braze	[breiz]	vt. 铜焊
bronze	[brɔnz]	n. 青铜；adj. 青铜色的

brunt	[brʌnt]	n. 冲击，冲势
bundle	['bʌndl]	n. 捆，束，包；v. 捆扎
burst	[bə:st]	v. 爆裂，爆发；n. 爆发，脉冲
bush	[buʃ]	n. 衬套
bushing	['buʃiŋ]	n. 轴衬，衬套
bypass	['baipɑ:s]	n. 旁路；vt. 设旁路，迂回
cable	['keibl]	n. 绳，缆，钢索
caliper	['kælipə]	n. 碟形制动器
canister	['kænistə]	n. 小罐，筒
capacitor	[kə'pæsitə]	n. 电容器
carb	[kɑ:b]	n. 化油器
carbon	['kɑ:bən]	n. 碳
centerline	['sentəlain]	n. 中心线
chain	[tʃein]	n. 链（条）
charcoal	['tʃɑ:kəul]	n. 木炭
charge	[tʃɑ:dʒ]	n. 负荷，电荷，费用，充电
choke	[tʃəuk]	n. 窒息，阻气门
chrome	[krəum]	n. 铬，铬合金
circuit	['sə:kit]	n. 电路，一圈
circular	['sə:kjulə]	adj. 圆形的，循环的
circulate	['sə:kjuleit]	v. （使）流通，（使）运行，（使）循环
circumference	[sə'kʌmfərəns]	n. 圆周，周围
clamp	[klæmp]	vt. 夹住，夹紧
classify	['klæsifai]	vt. 分类，分级
clearance	['kliərəns]	n. 清除
clog	[klɔg]	n. 木底鞋，障碍；v. 障碍，阻塞
clutch	[klʌtʃ]	n. 离合器
coasting	['kəustiŋ]	n. 滑行，惯性运动
collapse	[kə'læps]	n. 倒塌，崩溃；vi. 倒塌，崩溃，瓦解
collar	['kɔlə]	n. 法兰盘，联轴节，轴衬，环
communication	[kə,mju:ni'keiʃn]	n. 信息，通讯
compact	['kɔmpækt]	adj. 紧凑的，紧密的，简洁的
compensate	['kɔmpənseit]	v. 偿还，补偿，付报酬
component	[kəm'pəunənt]	n. 成分；adj. 组成的，构成的
compound	['kɔmpaund]	n. 混合物，化合物
comprise	[kəm'praiz]	vt. 包括，由…组成
compromise	['kɔmprəmaiz]	n. 妥协，折衷；v. 妥协，折衷
concave	['kɔn'keiv]	adj. 凹的，凹入的；n. 凹，凹面
condenser	[kən'densə]	n. 电容器
conjunction	[kən'dʒʌŋkʃən]	n. 联合，关联，连接词

conquer	[ˈkɔŋkə]	vt. 征服，战胜，克服
consequently	[ˈkɔnsikwəntli]	adv. 从而，因此
considerable	[kənˈsidərəbl]	adj. 相当大的，值得考虑的，相当可观的
constantly	[ˈkɔnstəntli]	adv. 不变地，经常地
controller	[kənˈtrəulə]	n. 控制器，调节器，擦纵器
coolant	[ˈkuːlənt]	n. 冷冻剂，冷却液
coordinate	[kəuˈɔːdinit]	vt. 调整，整理
coordination	[kəuˌɔːdiˈneiʃən]	n. 同等，调和
copper	[ˈkɔpə]	n. 铜
correspond	[kɔrisˈpɔnd]	vi. 符合，协调，通信，相当，相应
countless	[ˈkautlis]	adj. 无数的，数不尽的
crank	[kræŋk]	n. 曲柄；v. 起动
crown	[kraun]	n. 王冠，花冠，顶
curl	[kəːl]	v. （使）卷曲
curve	[kəːv]	vt. 弯，使弯曲
deceleration	[diːseləˈreiʃən]	n. 减速，熄灭
demonstrate	[ˈdemənstreit]	vt. 示范，证明，论证
dependable	[diˈpendəbl]	adj. 可靠的，可信的
deplete	[diˈpliːt]	vt. 耗尽，使衰竭
desirable	[diˈzaiərəbl]	adj. 值得要的，合意的
destination	[destiˈneiʃən]	n. 目的地，终点
destruct	[disˈtrʌkt]	vi. 破坏
detect	[diˈtekt]	vt. 察觉，发觉，探测
deteriorate	[diˈtiəriəreit]	v. （使）恶化
differential	[difəˈreʃəl]	n. 差速器
diode	[ˈdaiəud]	n. 二极管
discrete	[disˈkriːt]	adj. 不连续的，离散的
disengage	[disinˈgeidʒ]	v. 分离，断开，切断
distinct	[disˈtiŋkt]	adj. 清楚的，明显的，独特的
distribute	[disˈtribju(ː)t]	vt. 分发，分配，分区；v. 分发
domed	[dəumd]	adj. 有穹顶的，半球形的
droplet	[ˈdrɔplit]	n. 小滴
duct	[dʌkt]	n. 管，输送管
durable	[ˈdjuərəbl]	adj. 持久的，耐用的
eccentric	[ikˈsentrik]	adj. 古怪的
electrical	[iˈlektrik(ə)l]	adj. 电的，有关电的
electromotive	[ilektrəuˈməutiv]	adj. 电测的
eliminate	[iˈlimineit]	vt. 排除，消除；v. 除去
emission	[iˈmiʃən]	n. 散发，发射，喷射，排放
endure	[inˈdjuə]	v. 耐久，忍耐

energize	[ˈenədʒaiz]	vt. 使活跃，给与…电压
engage	[inˈgeidʒ]	vi. 接合，啮合
enormous	[iˈnɔːməs]	adj. 巨大的，庞大的
enrichment	[inˈritʃmənt]	n. 丰富，浓缩
equation	[iˈkweiʃən]	n. 相等，平衡，因素，等式
essential	[iˈsenʃəl]	adj. 本质的，主要的，最重要的
evenly	[ˈiːvənli]	adv. 均匀地，平坦地
eventually	[iˈventjuəli]	adv. 最后，终于
evolve	[iˈvɔlv]	v. （使）发展，（使）进展
existence	[igˈzistəns]	n. 存在，存在物
expectancy	[ikˈspektənsi]	n. 期待，期望
extract	[iksˈtrækt]	vt. 拔出，榨取，吸取
faithfully	[ˈfeiθfuli]	adv. 忠诚地，如实地，切实遵守地
feasible	[ˈfiːzəbl]	adj. 可行的，切实可行的
feedback	[ˈfiːdbæk]	n. 反馈，反应
fiberglass	[ˈfaibəglɑːs]	n. 玻璃纤维，玻璃丝
firmly	[ˈfəːmli]	adv. 坚定地，稳固地
flatten	[ˈflætn]	vt. 使平，变平
flexibility	[fleksəˈbiliti]	n. 柔韧，易弯曲，弹性
flexible	[ˈfleksəbl]	adj. 柔韧性，柔软的，能变形的
forge	[fɔːdʒ]	v. 铸造，伪造
gearbox	[giəbɔks]	n. 齿轮箱，变速箱
gearset	[ˈgiəset]	n. 齿轮组，变速箱
gearshift	[giəʃift]	n. 换挡，变速器
geometry	[dʒiˈɔmitri]	n. 几何学
grant	[grɑːnt]	vt. 同意，准予，承认
grill	[gril]	n. 烤架，铁格子，格栅
groove	[gruːv]	n. 凹槽
hesitation	[ˌheziˈteiʃən]	n. 犹豫，踌躇
hinge	[hindʒ]	vt. 装铰链
hydraulic	[haiˈdrɔːlik]	adj. 液压的
hydrogen	[ˈhaidrəudʒən]	n. 氢
hydrostatic	[haidrɔˈstætik]	adj. 液压静力的，流体静力的
idle	[ˈaidl]	vi. 空转，怠速
immerse	[iˈməːs]	v. 浸入，浸渍，泡
impeller	[imˈpelə]	n. 推进者，叶轮，泵轮
inadequate	[inˈædikwit]	adj. 不充分的，不适当的
induce	[inˈdjuːs]	vt. 促使，导致，引起
infinitely	[ˈinfinitli]	adv. 无限地，无穷地
infrared	[ˈinfrəˈred]	adj. 红外线的

ingest	[in'dʒest]	vt. 摄取，咽下，吸收
inhibiter	[in'hibitə]	n. 抑制剂，抑制者
initial	[i'niʃəl]	adj. 最初的，词首的，初始的
injection	[in'dʒekʃən]	n. 注射，喷射
innovation	[,inəu'veiʃən]	n. 改革，创新
install	[in'stɔ:l]	v. 安装，装配
insulate	['insjuleit]	vt. 使绝缘，隔离
interconnect	[,intə(:)kə'nekt]	vt. 使互相连接
intermittent	[,intə(:)'mitənt]	adj. 间歇的，断断续续的
interrupt	[intə'rʌpt]	vt. 阻断，阻止，打扰
intersect	[,intə'sekt]	vi. （直线）相交，交叉
intersection	[,intə(:)'sekʃən]	n. 十字路口，交叉点
irritating	['iriteitiŋ]	adj. 刺激的
isolate	['aisəleit]	vt. 分离，断开
journal	['dʒə:nl]	n. 定期刊物，杂志，轴颈，枢轴
Jupiter	['dʒu:pitə]	n. 木星
knob	[nɔb]	n. 球形捏手，球形突出物，旋钮
lap	[læp]	vi. 重叠，围住；vt. 包围，使重叠
latch	[lætʃ]	n. 门插销
layshaft	['leiʃɑ:ft]	n. 副轴，侧轴，中间轴
lever	['li:və, 'levə]	n. 杆，杠杆，控制杆
liable	['laiəbl]	adj. 易…的，有…倾向的，很有可能的
likelihood	['laiklihud]	n. 可能，可能性
lining	['lainiŋ]	n. 衬片，衬垫
lower	['ləuə]	vt. 放下，降下，减弱，贬低
magnet	['mægnit]	n. 磁体，磁铁
maintain	[men'tein]	vt. 维持，维修
majority	[mə'dʒɔriti]	n. 多数，大半
malfunction	[mæl'fʌŋkʃən]	n. 不正常起动，故障，出错
Mars	[mɑ:z]	n. 火星
mass	[mæs]	n. 块，大多数，质量，大量
mesh	[meʃ]	n. 啮合；vt. 啮合，编织
metallic	[mi'tælik]	adj. 金属（性）的
mileage	['mailidʒ]	n. 汽车消耗 1 加仑汽油所行驶的平均里程 [1 加仑（英）为 4.546dm^3]
millisecond	['mili,sekənd]	n. 毫秒
mimic	['mimik]	vt. 模仿，模拟
misfire	['mis'faiə]	v. 失火
mold	[məuld]	n. 模子，铸型；vt. 浇铸，塑造
momentarily	['məuməntərili]	adv. 即刻

monitor	['mɔnitə]	vt. 监控
motionless	['məuʃənis]	adj. 不动的，静止的，固定的
multiply	['mʌltipli]	v. 繁殖，乘，增加
nerve	[nə:v]	n. 神经，胆量，勇气
neutral	['nju:trəl]	n. 空挡
nickel	['nikl]	n. 镍
non-synchronous	[nɔn'siŋkrənəs]	adj. 非同步的，异步的，不同期的
notched	[nɔtʃt]	adj. 有凹口的，有锯齿状的
noticeably	['nəutisəbli]	adv. 易见地，显著地
nozzle	['nɔzl]	n. 管口，喷嘴
octane	['ɔktein]	n. 辛烷
optical	['ɔptikəl]	adj. 光学的
ordinary	['ɔ:dinəri]	adj. 正常的，规定的
oval	['əuvəl]	adj. 卵形的，椭圆的
overdrive	['əuvə'draiv]	vt. 超速传动
oxygen	['ɔksidʒən]	n. 氧
passage	['pæsidʒ]	n. 通过，经过，通道
pavement	['peivmənt]	n. 人行道，公路
pellet	['pelit]	n. 小球
periodic	[piəri'ɔdik]	adj. 周期的，定期的
perpendicular	[,pə:pən'dikjulə]	adj. 垂直的，正交的；n. 垂线
persistent	[pə'sistənt]	adj. 持久稳固的
pinion	['pinjən]	n. 小齿轮
pitch	[pitʃ]	n. 程度
pivot	['pivət]	n. 枢轴；vi. 在枢轴上转动
plumbing	['plʌmiŋ]	n. 管道，导管
plunger	['plʌndʒə]	n. 活塞，柱塞
poisonous	['pɔiznəs]	adj. 有毒的
port	[pɔ:t]	n. 港口，舱门，端口
precise	[pri'sais]	adj. 精确的，准确的；n. 精确
premature	[,premə'tjuə]	adj. 未成熟的，太早的，早熟的
preset	['pri:'set]	vt. 事先调整
project	['prɔdʒekt]	n. 计划，方案；v. 设计，计划，发射
property	['prɔpəti]	n. 性能，特性
proportion	[prə'pɔ:ʃən]	n. 比例，部分
protrude	[prə'tru:d]	v. 突出
pulley	['puli]	n. 皮带轮，滑轮
rack	[ræk]	n. 架，齿条
radiator	['reidieitə]	n. 散热器，水箱
radius	['reidjəs]	n. 半径

recess	[ri'ses]	vt. 使凹进
recharge	[ri:'tʃɑːdʒ]	vt. 再充电
reciprocating	[ri'siprəkeitiŋ]	adj. 往复的，来回的，交替的，摆动的
recirculate	[ri'sə:kjuleit]	v. 再通行，再流通
recommend	[rekə'mend]	vt. 推荐，介绍
rectifier	['rektifaiə]	n. 纠正者，整顿者，校正者，整流器
refine	[ri'fain]	vt. 精炼，精制，精选，改进
reflect	[ri'flekt]	v. 反射，反映
regulator	['regjuleitə]	n. 调整者，校准者，调整器
relay	['ri:lei]	n. 继电器
reliability	[ri,laiə'biliti]	n. 可靠性
reliable	[ri'laiəbl]	adj. 可靠的，安全的
relieve	[ri'li:v]	vt. 减轻，解除，援救
remote	[ri'məut]	adj. 遥远的
requirement	[ri'kwaiəmənt]	n. 需求，要求
reserve	[ri'zə:v]	n. 储备（物），储藏量；vt. 储备，保存
reservoir	['rezəvwɑ:]	n. 蓄水池，储存器
resistance	[ri'zistəns]	n. 反抗，抵抗，阻力，电阻
resistant	[ri'zistənt]	adj. 抵抗的，有抵抗力的
resistor	[ri'zistə]	n. 电阻器
respectively	[ri'spektivli]	adv. 分别地，各个地
responsible	[ris'pɔnsəbl]	adj. 有责任的，可靠的，可依赖的
retract	[ri'trækt]	v. 缩回，缩进，收回
retractable	[ri'træktəbl]	adj. 可收回的
reverse	[ri'və:s]	n. 倒挡，倒退；vt. 颠倒，倒转
ridge	[ridʒ]	n. 背脊，峰，隆起线
rim	[rim]	n. 边缘，边沿，胎环
rocker	['rɔkə]	n. 摇杆
rollover	['rəul,əuvə]	n. 翻滚
rotational	[rəu'teiʃənəl]	adj. 转动的，循环的
rotor	['rəutə]	n. 转子，回转轴，转动体
route	[ru:t]	n. 路线，路程，通道；v. 发送
routine	[ru:'ti:n]	n. 常规，日常事务，程序
rub	[rʌb]	v. 擦，摩擦
saturated	['sætʃəreitid]	adj. 渗透的，饱和的，深颜色的
scheme	[ski:m]	n. 设计图，方案，系统
seesaw	['si:sɔ:]	n. 秋千
sense	[sens]	vt. 感到，理解，认识
sequential	[si'kwinʃəl]	adj. 连续的，相续的，有顺序的
serpentine	['sə:pəntain]	adj. 弯曲的

servo	['sə:vəu]	n. 伺服，伺服系统
shell	[ʃel]	n. 壳，外形
shifter	['ʃiftə]	n. 变速杆
shutter	['ʃʌtə]	n. 关闭者，百叶窗
simplify	['simplifai]	vt. 单一化，简单化
skidding	[skidiŋ]	adj. 滑动的，滑溜的，打滑的
slap	[slæp]	n. 拍，掌击，拍击声
slippery	[slipəri]	adj. 滑的，光滑的
slosh	[slɔʃ]	n. 泥泞，溅泼声；v. 溅，泼
solenoid	['səulinɔid]	n. 螺线管
specific	[spi'sifik]	n. 细节；adj. 精确的，明确的，特殊的
spill	[spil]	n. 溢出（量），溅出（量）；vt. 使溢出，使散落
spin	[spin]	v. 旋转，纺，纺纱；n. 旋转
spindle	['spindl]	n. 轴，心轴
split	[split]	n. 裂口，裂痕；v.（使）裂开，分裂
spongy	['spʌndʒi]	adj. 像海绵的，柔软的
spray	[sprei]	n. 喷雾，飞沫；vt. 喷射，喷溅
squeak	[skwi:k]	n. 尖叫声；v. 发出尖叫声
squeal	[skwi:l]	n. 尖叫声，振鸣声
squeegee	['skwi:dʒi:]	n. 橡胶扫帚，橡胶滚轴
squirt	[skwə:t]	v. 喷出
starter	['stɑ:tə]	n. 起动机
static	['stætik]	adj. 静态的；n. 静电干扰
stationary	['steiʃ(ə)nəri]	adj. 固定的
stator	['steitə]	n. 定子，固定片，导轮
steady	['stedi]	adj. 稳定的，平稳的，持续的
stem	[stem]	n. 茎，干
stick	[stik]	v. 粘住，粘贴；vt. 刺，戳
strand	[strænd]	n. 线，绳
strip	[strip]	vt. 剥，剥去；n. 条，带
suction	['sʌkʃən]	n. 吸入，吸力，吸引，抽吸装置
suffer	['sʌfə]	vt. 遭受，经历；vi. 受痛苦，受损害
sufficiently	[sə'fiʃəntli]	adv. 十分地，充分地
suitable	['sju:təbl]	adj. 适当的，相配的
suppress	[sə'pres]	vt. 镇压，抑制，使止住
surely	['ʃuəli]	adj. 的确，当然
susceptible	[sə'septəbl]	adj. 易受影响的，易感动的，容许……的
synthetic	[sin'θetik]	adj. 合成的，人造的，综合的
tandem	['tændəm]	adv. 一前一后

tap	[tæp]	*vt.* 轻打，轻敲
tear	[tiə]	*vi.* 撕破，被撕破
technician	[tek'niʃən]	*n.* 技术人员
thermostat	['θə:məstæt]	*n.* 节温器，温度调节装置
thread	[θred]	*n.* 螺纹
threshold	['θreʃhəuld]	*n.* 开始，开端，极限
throttle	['θrɔtl]	*v.* 扼杀
throughout	[θru(:)'aut]	*prep.* 遍及，贯穿；*adv.* 到处，始终
tightly	['taitli]	*adv.* 紧紧地，坚固地
tin	[tin]	*n.* 锡；*adj.* 锡制的
trailer	['treilə]	*n.* 追踪者，拖车
trait	[treit]	*n.* 显著的特点，特性
transformer	[træns'fɔ:mə]	*n.* 变压器
transmission	[trænz'miʃən]	*n.* 传动，传送
transmit	[trænz'mit]	*vt.* 传输，传达，传播
transparent	[træns'pɛərent]	*adj.* 透明的，半透明的
trigger	['trigə]	*vt.* 引发，引起，触发
turbine	['tə:bin, -bain]	*n.* 涡轮
turbo	['tə:bəu]	*n.* 涡轮，增压涡轮
twist	[twist]	*vt.* 拧，扭曲；*vi.* 扭弯，扭曲
typically	['tipikəli]	*adv.* 代表性地，作为特色地
undergo	[ʌndə'gəu]	*vt.* 经历，遭受，忍受
unitized	['ju:nitaizd]	*adj.* 组成的，合成的，成套的
untwist	['ʌn'twist]	*v.* 拆开，解开
unusable	[ʌn'ju:zəbl]	*adj.* 不可用的，不能使用的
utilize	[ju:'tilaiz]	*vt.* 利用
vane	[vein]	*n.* 翼，叶片
variable	['vɛəriəbl]	*n.* 变量，变数
version	['və:ʃən]	*n.* 形式，种类
via	['vaiə, 'vi:ə]	*prep.* 经，通过，经由
visibility	[ˌvizi'biliti]	*n.* 可见度，能见度
volatility	[ˌvɔlə'tiliti]	*n.* 挥发性
voltmeter	['vəultˌmi:tə(r)]	*n.* 伏特计
wax	[wæks]	*n.* 蜡，蜡状物
wear	[wer]	*vt.* 穿，戴；*v.* 磨损，用旧
whirl	[(h)wə:l]	*v.* （使）旋转，急动，急走
wipe	[waip]	*v.* 擦，擦去 *n.* 擦，拭
withdraw	[wið'drɔ:]	*vt.* 收回，撤销；*v.* 撤退
wrap	[ræp]	*vt.* 包装，卷，缠绕
zigzag	['zigzæg]	*v.* 成 Z 字形，曲折前进

Phrases and Expressions

a split second	一瞬间，一刹那
accelerator pump	加速泵
air conditioning compressor	空调压缩机
air cooled	风冷
align with	与……结盟
alloy steel	合金钢
alternating current（AC）	交流电
anti-lock brake system	防抱死制动系统
as well as	也，又
aside from	除了，除……以外
at all times	无论何时，一直
at the same time	同时
back up light	倒车灯
battery cable	蓄电池电缆
be about to	即将
be known as	被认为是
be subject to	遭受……
because of	由于
belt tensioner	皮带张紧器
bleed off	放出，排出
body controller	车身控制单元
brake band	制动带
brake fluid	制动液，刹车油
brake pad	制动快，制动衬垫
brake pedal	制动踏板
call for	要求，请求
cam follower	挺柱
camshaft position sensor	凸轮轴位置传感器
carbon and hydrogen compound	碳氢化合物
catalytic converter	催化转换器
centrifugal advance	离心提前
centrifugal force	离心力

charcoal canister	炭罐
charging system	充电系统
clear away	清除，消失
closed loop control	闭环控制
clutch disc	离合器从动盘
cog-type belt	齿型带
compression ratio	压缩比
compression ring	压缩环
connecting rod	连杆
control module	控制模块
coolant temperature sensor	冷却液温度传感器
cooling system	冷却系统
crankshaft position sensor	曲轴位置传感器
cylinder bore	气缸，缸径
cylinder wall	气缸壁
depend on	依靠，依赖
devote to	专心于，致力于
diaphragm pump	膜片泵
diaphragm spring	膜片弹簧
direct current（DC）	直流电
disk brake	盘式制动器，碟刹
distributor cam	分电器凸轮
distributor cap	分电器盖
distributor housing	分电器壳体
distributor rotor	分火头
distributor shaft	分电器轴
distributorless ignition system	无分电器点火系统
door handle	门把手
drag link	转向直拉杆
drive shaft	传动轴
drum brake	鼓式制动器
dry friction clutch	干式摩擦离合器
dual overhead camshaft	双顶置凸轮轴
electro magnet	电磁铁
electromotive force	电动势
electronic circuit	电子电路
electronic ignition system	电子点火系统
engine compartment	发动机舱
engine control unit	发动机控制单元
engine speed sensor	发动机转速传感器

ethylene glycol	乙烯乙二醇
evaporative emission control	燃油蒸发控制
exhaust gas recirculation system	废气再循环系统
exhaust valve	排气门
external spline	外花键
fan belt	风扇皮带
fan blade	风扇叶片
feeler gauge	塞尺
fixed contact point	固定触点
fluid coupling	液力偶合器
forward gear	前进挡
front axle	前桥，前轴
fuel filter	燃油滤清器
fuel injection system	燃油喷射系统
fuel pump	燃油泵
fuel tank	燃油箱
gas pedal	油门踏板
gear ratio	齿数比，齿轮传动比
governor valve	调速阀
heater core	加热器
high energy ignition（HEI）	高能点火
high-strength steel	高强度钢
high-tension wire	高压线
idle circuit	怠速系统
ignition coil	点火线圈
ignition switch	点火开关
in a hurry	匆忙
in a matter of	大约，大概
in conjunction with	与……协力，与……联合
in excess of	超过
in fact	事实上
in operation	操作中，运转中
in other words	换句话说
in relation to	关于，涉及，与……相比
in use	在使用着
inlet valve	进气门
instead of	代替，而不是……
internal combustion engine	内燃机
keep away from	远离
keep from	防止……

keyless-entry remote control	无钥匙强入系统
king pin	主销
lap over	重叠
limit switch	限位开关
linear motion	线性运动
liquid cooled	水冷
lock up	闭锁，锁住，固定
lockout switch	锁止开关
magnetic field	磁场
main bearing	主轴承
main circuit	主供油系统
make contact with	和……接触
manifold absolute pressure sensor	进气歧管压力传感器
manual transmission	手动变速器
manual valve	手控阀
mass airflow sensor	空气流量传感器
master cylinder	主缸
mechanical ignition system	机械点火系统
movable contact point	移动触点
multiple plate friction clutch	多片式摩擦离合器
neutral safety switch	空挡安全开关
nothing more that	不过，不外乎
oil pressure	油压，机油压力
oil ring	油环
on the drawing board	在设计阶段，在筹划之中
on the order of	属于……一类的，与……相似的
one-way valve	单向阀
optical sensor	光学传感器，光敏元件
overhead valve	顶置气门
oxygen sensor	氧传感器
parking brake	驻车制动
permanent magnet	永久磁铁
pickup coil	传感线圈
pin boss	销孔座
piston pin	活塞销
piston ring	活塞环
pitman arm	转向摇臂
planet gear	行星轮
planet gear carrier	行星架
planetary gearset	行星齿轮组

power brake booster	真空助力器
power Door Lock	动力门锁
power enrichment circuit	加浓系统
power steering	动力转向
power window	动力车窗
pressure plate	压盘
pressure regulator	压力调节器
pressure-relief valve	卸压阀
primary circuit	初级电路
primary winding	初级绕组
push rod	推杆
rack and pinion steering gear	齿轮齿条式转向器
radiator cap	散热器盖
rear-axle housing	后桥壳，后轴壳
rearview mirror	后视镜
recirculating ball steering gear	循环球式转向器
rectifier assembly	整流器
refer to	谈到，涉及，查询，参考
relative to	相对，相关
release fork	释放叉，分离叉
reserve tank	膨胀水箱
reverse gear	倒挡
ring gear	齿圈，齿环
ring groove	环槽
ring land	环岸
rocker arm	摇臂
rotary valve	旋转阀
rotary vane pump	旋转叶片泵
secondary circuit	次级电路
secondary coil	次级线圈
secondary winding	次级绕组
shift lever	换挡杆
shift valve	换挡阀
single plate friction clutch	单片式摩擦离合器
slip ring	滑环
so far	迄今，至今
spark plug	火花塞
speed sensor	速度传感器
spline shaft	花键轴
spool valve	伺服阀

spur gear	直齿轮
starter relay	起动继电器
starter solenoid	起动机电磁线圈
steering arm	转向摇臂
steering column	转向柱，转向杆
steering gear	转向器
steering knuckle	转向节
steering shaft	转向柱，转向杆
steering wheel	方向盘
step up	走近，逐步增加，提升，提高
stick up	竖起，突起
such as	比如
sun gear	太阳轮
SUV (sport utility vehicle)	运动型多用途车
switch to	转到，换到
synthetic rubber	合成橡胶
take over	接替
threaded hole	螺纹孔
threaded rod	螺杆
throttle body	节气门体
throttle plate	节气门
throttle position sensor	节气门位置传感器
throttle valve	节气门阀
throw-out bearing	分离轴承，推力轴承
tie rod	转向横拉杆
time interval	时间间隔
timing belt	正时皮带
timing gear	正时齿轮
tooth pitch	齿距
torque converter	液力变矩器
torsion bar	扭力杆
vacuum advance	真空提前
vacuum modulator valve	真空调节阀
valve body	阀体
valve mechanism	气门机构
valve overlap	气门重叠
valve seat	气门座
valve timing	气门正时
vapor lock	气阻
voltage regulator	电压调节器

voltage sensor	电压传感器
water pump	水泵
wear out	磨损，用坏，用旧
window-switch control panel	车窗开关控制面板
windshield wiper	挡风玻璃刮雨器
wiper blade	雨刮片
wiring harness	线束
worm gear	涡轮

Reference

［1］ 蒋芳，吴喜骊. 汽车专业英语 ［M］. 北京：机械工业出版社，2009.

［2］ 王木林. 汽车商务英语 ［M］. 北京：化学工业出版社，2009.

［3］ 丁继斌，张海宁. 汽车专业英语 ［M］. 北京：机械工业出版社，2014.

［4］ 刘璇，于秀敏. 实用汽车英语 ［M］. 北京：北京理工大学出版社，2008.